A Blind Date With the World

The Great Global Scavenger Hunt

William D. Chalmers

Writers Club Press

San Jose New York Lincoln Shanghai

A Blind Date With The World
The Great Global Scavenger Hunt

Published by Writers Club Press
an imprint of iUniverse.com, Inc.

For information address:
iUniverse.com, Inc.
620 North 48th Street
Suite 201
Lincoln, NE 68504-3467
www.iuniverse.com

ISBN: 0-595-09622-0

Printed in the United States of America

To my mother and father who opened the doors to the world for me. Thank you.

I miss you...

"Oh, East is East, and West is West, and never the twain shall meet,
Till Earth and Sky stand presently at God's great Judgement Seat;
But there is neither East nor West, border, nor breed, nor birth,
When two strong men face to face,
though they come from ends of the earth!"

Rudyard Kipling, 1889

"Imagine there's no countries,
It isn't hard to do.
Nothing to kill or die for,
and no religions too."

John Lennon, 1971

Contents

In The Immortal Steps of Stanley and Livingston...
Or, is it Hope and Crosby? 1

Changes in Latitude=Changes in Attitude 11

A Journey Without Maps 37

The Past Being Prologue 55

Bali Ha'i, circa 1989 65

Dawn Came Early, and Other Stupid
Opening Lines... 83

Quotes From A Street Vendor 113

Missing...But Presumed To Be Having
A Good Time? 133

Going Nowhere Fast! 163

Lawyers, Guns and Money in New York City 177

Back to the Rat Race 191

The Human*Race* 1989: The Slightly Abridged Version 199

List of Tables

Anonymous Travel Collections… 13

Wonders of the Middle World 54

Restaurant Eating Tips 66

Great Islands 72

Natural Wonders Of The World 90

Great Shopping Districts 117

Wonders Of The Ancient World 127

The 10 Commandments of Travel 137

Wonders Of The Modern World 141

Great Boat Rides 159

Top HumanRace Memories 192

Foreword

1989. Do you remember what life was like back then? Just twelve years ago as I write this, but seemingly another lifetime ago. Well, that's the milieu that this grand adventure you are about to embark on was undertaken. It was a time when the Berlin Wall and the Soviet Union still existed. A time when apartheid was the law of the land in South Africa and the Palestinians had no land to call their own. A time when Magic Johnson's Lakers were trying to *three-peat* and the Great Gretzky was performing nightly in Los Angeles. A time before e-mail, or e-*anything* for that matter, when the world was split between competing global ideologies of the Cold War. Before the entire Clinton-Gore era, HMO's, Operation Desert Storm and Millennium Madness. Before *Prozac*, *Viagra* and *Wonderbras*. (In that order!) Nasty fellows like Boesky, Milken, Trump and North made the *Headline News*, while Havel was a dissident and Mandela was serving 25 to life in prison.

The HumanRace was held between October 17th when the Loma Prieta earthquake wrecked havoc on the Bay area and November 9th when the Berlin Wall fell, signaling the end of the Cold War. Historic times indeed! I began writing my recollections immediately after returning home from the HumanRace around Thanksgiving 1989 and finished it over the Winter. And like many of my other creative endeavors, it sat on a shelf ever since. It was written in the spirit of the times, the late 1980's. It was written by someone who hadn't yet married and then separated, hadn't had kids to call his own, hadn't yet graduated from a 12-step program (*Travelers Anonymous*), discovered yoga and

Buddhism, and hadn't really taken his writing career too seriously. (Sorry!) Indeed, I hadn't yet stopped acting like a big kid playing in the world with little or no real responsibilities. It was indeed a very different era for all of us.

The things I have written about all seemed true at the time and I really can't apologize for any of those observances, view points and acts of silliness. What I have written, I have written. So when I finally decided, after a decade of urging by family and friends to publish this grueling travel adventure chronicle, I decided not to edit or censure any of my words of wisdom. Nor have I added any insights or knowledge that I have accumulated since 1989. Political correctness be damned! I say this now because, at times this manuscript is not pretty on several levels. What I do seek is understanding and compassion from the reader, who may find something offensive in the this book. It was not my intent at the time, nor is it twelve years later, to cause anyone any harm. And so I offer you this travelogue and let the chips fall where they may, trusting that everyone will understand both the times and the author.

As I re-read what I've just written, I can almost hear a politician running for President saying: "*Well, I did experiment with it once in college. I didn't really enjoy it and have never done it since. It was a youthful indiscretion that I have truly regretted ever since...*" Yeah, that's what I'm trying to say here. The 1980's were fun times at the Height of the American Empire in the Greed is Good decade, so fuck 'em if they can't take a joke! Nuff said. Enjoy...

Acknowledgements

I am a very grateful guy and I have a lot to be thankful for.

First, I want to of course thank all those that were part of the 1989 Human*Race*, JB and the other event organizers, the corporate sponsors, the participants (You were all great fun to travel and compete with!) and the wonderful people we met out on the road. Everyone added a little something to the cocktail, be it bitter or sweets.

I want to thank my best friend Andy Valvur, who's been my intrepid travel partner since 1984. Thanks for getting me through this and all of our great global misadventures.

I want to thank my girlfriend at the time of the race, Alla Sigga Jonsdottir, for allowing me to indulge in such a global affair of the heart.

I want to thank my good friend Neil Breton for giving me the opportunity to fulfill a dream and believing in me when I told him in September 1989 that, "*there's absolutely no doubt in my mind that we will win this race.*"

I want to thank those that helped me edit this manuscript and ready it for publication. Especially Pamela L. Finmark, whose fresh bright eyes helped me see things I hadn't seen in many years and who brought new meaning to the great literary question of the day: "Who's your libel attorney?" and "What university did you say you graduated from?" Thank you Pamela.

I want to thank my precious little girl Petra Luna, who's growing up way too fast, for understanding all the times when Poppi says he's working and needs another minute before he can come and play *Barbie* with her. I love you sweets. Here I come...

Thank you all for buying this damn once-upon-a-time labor of love!

In The Immortal Steps of Stanley and Livingston...
Or, *is it Hope and Crosby?*

I remember exactly what time it was when I realized that this was not going to be your normal, everyday, run-of-the-mill around-the-world trip. I remember because moments earlier I had been roused from my sleep by the piercing blast of an air horn from a logging truck bearing down on our mechanically feeble mini-bus. I don't know why this particular one woke me as I'd been hearing the thunder of these logging truck horns all night. Perhaps it was the urgency I felt from the blower's end. This was followed immediately by a lightning quick vehicular move that can best be described as evasive action, a buffeting of our severely cramped bus by something really big, going really fast, really close. It must have been a near miss because our normally unflappable driver responded with reciprocal blasts from his horn and a stream of bloody epithets.

One thing about people and swearing, it's universal. No matter what country you're in, it has the same rhythm and tone, and right now it was being delivered in some sort of remote Javanese mountain tribe dialect. Wide awake, my illuminating digital watch informed me that it was precisely 3:47 a.m. WIT, *Western Indonesian Time*. My traveling partner slept on, blissfully unaware of yet another brush with disaster. This near death experience was shared only by myself and the gaunt Indonesian at the wheel, though judging by the last eleven hours, my idea of a near death experience was just another night's work for our driver.

Then, I heard yet another sickening thud. My unofficial road-kill count had climbed to nine!

The time was easy. The location, where the hell were we? Well, that was another story. On board an overbooked mini-bus with twelve passengers and one goat was a gimme. Geographically though? Well, near as I could figure, somewhere on the island of Java, due east of Krakatoa, I presumed. I finally had to admit that this was not your typical vacation, where all you had to do, aside from wearing an obligatory collection of multi-colored plastic beads around your neck, oily gobs of asbestos-based *SPF*-45, a fashionably tight-fitting jet-black *Speedo*, and continuously suck down frozen double daiquiris at some Yuppie *Club Med*-like beach resort in the deep blue waters of the Caribbean. Of course, right about now, an extra-strong peach daiquiri sounded pretty good to me!

A few hours earlier we'd passed through a seemingly prehistoric village, whose name I couldn't spell, and whose hollow black dot didn't appear anywhere in my usually trusty *Baedeker*. And then I remembered, that maps don't lie, *map makers do*! There we'd graciously been given a much needed respite from our kidney punishing, eighteen hour *SRO* bus ride. A rest from the perils of rocketing down rugged volcano-laden terrain on unmarked gravel roads barely wide enough for two *Yugo*'s to pass. It was noted, that somewhere around here, wherever here was, if legend proved correct, and we seriously questioned our source's anthropological credibility, headhunters lurked. And not the kind that conduct nationwide executive talent searches either. Despite the source, I inconspicuously checked up on the region's tribal and religious holiday schedule.

Contemplating our dubious good fortune, as I shifted my now numb body from one uncomfortable sleeping position to another, I waxed philosophically that this is what living on the edge is all about.

The *edge*, wise men say, is when you're truly alive and experiencing life to its absolute fullest. That is, enjoying the benefits of all of your senses. Others may differ, but in my humble opinion, it occurs while participating in one of only four human activities: When you're in the heat of battle; letting it all ride on the craps table; impassioned in the throes of wildly uninhibited sex, which come to think of it is pretty much like battle! And finally, when you're traveling without the benefit of a prearranged itinerary. Like we happened to be doing at the moment.

Some armchair pop psychologists mistakenly refer to these special moments of hyper-consciousness as peak experiences, or better yet, totally self-absorbed flows. No matter, time was standing still for us, and we were definitely sitting on the edge, in the front row center stage of life.

My travel partner and best friend, Andy Valvur, and I were adventurous, *gung-ho* participants in an around-the-world souvenir-collecting odyssey via public transportation that was quickly turning us into cultural terrorists, as well as subjecting us to a grueling and exhausting marathon. And it seemed like we were about to hit that infamous wall of physical exhaustion, where we'd either catch our second wind long enough to survive and maybe even be victorious, or fall by the wayside totally humiliated like so many other wannabe contenders. The latter version had me envisioning a fat-assed Brando in some rundown bar telling somebody, no, make that anybody who'd listen, "*I coulda been a contender. I coulda been somebody.*" Well, we weren't going to let that happen to us, we were gonna be somebody, even if it killed us.

All total, Andy and I traveled approximately forty thousand strenuous miles in seventeen frenzied days through twenty-two world-class cities, and countless not so world-class villages, in ten countries scattered across four continents. Truly, a once-in-a-lifetime international adventure. Like cultural archeologists on speed, we pick-axed our way through dozens of ancient urban landscapes unearthing signs of intelligent life. Of course we fought and disagreed on numerous occasions, mostly about where and when to eat and where and when to sleep; Andy's a carnivore and a disgustingly cheerful morning person, whereas I'm more of a herbivore and hyperactive late night person.

We also had a few of those potential relationship ending: "But, I thought you were listening when she gave us those directions?" incidents. In spite of these unusual metabolic stresses and strains, and geopolitical trials and tribulations, we somehow kept our peculiar friendship wholly intact. We also collected an incredible triple-bonus frequent-flier mileage windfall on our multicultural extravaganza. We fondly came to describe this act of lunacy as our *Whirled Tour 1989*.

It all began one Sunday morning while I was perusing the usually predictable and tame *New York Times* Travel section (30 April 1989) on a plane to London. There, tucked away in the lower left hand column, was a tiny article hidden as a "Travel Advisory" seeking contestants for an international race. Billed as the Human*Race*, it was an around-the-world global scavenger hunt travel adventure that turned the whole world into our personal gameboard. The twist was that we and our fellow contestants were to be transformed into human chess pieces. As soon as I touched down in England for my get acquainted weekend date with an Icelandic blonde, I faxed the piece to Andy in New York and informed him that we were entering.

The contest was the illegitimate brainchild of a Southern Californian entrepreneur, hence forth known simply in these pages as JB, who was a radical Jewish hippie *cum* insurance salesman *cum* Texas-based commercial real estate developer *cum* international ethnic art dealer *cum* global gameshow host in his late forties. It was clear that JB had had a 1980's bypass operation along the way and that now he was clearly more than the sum of his numerous shady prior occupations. Nonetheless, he was now selling eccentric travel junkies, and with wealthy *Type-A* personalities suffering from incessant *affluenza*, a global ego-trip promising us the "*cultural experience of a lifetime.*"

We bought into it anyway.

So, from our respective cozy apartments, Andy in manic downtown Manhattan and me from laid-back West-Los Angeles, we set off on a seemingly never ending spin around our fascinating global village.

Along with enduring unforgettable physical hardships, we also suffered from periodic sieges of intellectual gridlock, where we quickly learned how to anticipate and tolerate the unexpected in about a dozen different dialects, most of which we didn't speak! Possessed with healthy spirits for travel and adventure, and relishing a good challenge when we saw one, and with a wide selection of *Visa, Mastercard,* and *American Express* gold cards; we set out from earthquake ravaged San Francisco in late October of 1989 on our grand world tour.

Our secret, though predetermined, race course was to take us in a West-to-East circumnavigation of our little blue-green planet. Despite JB's directional decree, some found it somewhat amusing how we started out in the mysterious and sultry Far East and ended up returning to psychotic New York City via freezing Western Europe. "Go figure," I told them not fully understanding the issue!?

At any rate, Valvur and Chalmers were about join, at least in our mind's eye, the likes of other historic wanderers such as *Lewis and Clark, Stanley and Livingston* or *Hope and Crosby.* Intrepid travelholics of our Baby Boomer generation.

Oh how perfectly romantic it all sounded. Oh how terribly tame it all seemed. A First Class travel adventure I thought to myself, envisioning exotic restaurants, five-star hotels, magnificent air conditioned tour buses and quiet airport lounges where tall cool drinks are served by hot-looking sarong clad Singapore Girls. "A champagne and caviar voyage around the world," my extremely jealous Icelandic girlfriend called it before I left.

"Yea, right!" I would later think while I listened to the air horns of large trucks in the Indonesian night…"Wonderful!" I muttered later while trying to grab a catnap in an ergonomically challenged luggage locker surrounded by drunks being rudely interrupted by snarling saber-toothed police dogs at 2 a.m. somewhere in the Italian Alps…"Great vacation!" I would mock repeatedly while eating a meal of questionable organic origin from the express window of *chez* street-vendor No. 23 somewhere in the remote highlands of Malaysia...

Believe me, our fantasy-based travel adventure notions were seen lickety-split flying away somewhere over Kuala Lumpur. Or was it Cairo? "Where's the *Kea Lani* Hotel when you need it?" I wondered after several sleepless nights. And just when I finally would drift into a restless slumber, Andy would rudely wake me and tell me I was whimpering in my sleep. "What did I say?" I asked. "Oh waiter, just a tad more *béarnaise* sauce please!" Andy replied.

I would daydream about junk food on board an Egyptian train heading into the searing desert whose dining car, and I use the term rather loosely here, served only tepid watered-down tea and snacks that consisted of sandwiches made of something that once might have been classified a meat by-product which our foul smelling steward pronounced "*saa-witch...saa-witch*" as he pushed his little squeaky wheeled cart down the aisle.

The guidelines of this globe-trotting game, and make no mistake about it, it was indeed a grown-up kids game, seemed simple enough. Although as I write this narrative dishonorable lawyers, barristers and solicitors, from several continents who all readily provide reasonable doubt at reasonable prices, are still attempting to legally decipher the elaborate rules and regulations, and gaping loopholes. And yet, after a lengthy alcohol fueled briefing we came to understand our Human*Race* tasks simply as:

1) *Locate the list of required scavenges.* Our translation: purchase specific cultural souvenirs, retaining the receipts of said purchases, while personally visiting a mind-boggling number of temples, palaces, cathedrals, shrines, museums, monuments, historical sites and assorted shopping malls, ah, I mean, *pasars* and bazaars;

2) *Document your presence.* Our legal interpretation: take a quick photo or two, depending on the instructions; and finally,

3) *Travel exclusively via public transportation.* We read: experience countless frustrating logistical *Amtrak*-like nightmares.

Worst of all though, after reading the small print, we learned that no private *Lear* jets or private guides were permitted. Nor were any high-tech specialized personal communications devices allowed. With sad, long faces, we left our cellular telephones, CIA-approved burst transmitter ordered from the back pages of *Soldier of Fortune* magazine, and with our *INMARSAT* satellite communication system, at home.

With our applications for entry into the Human*Race* accepted and our hefty $11,000 per team cover charge attached, we were now poised, however naively, to conquer the world and win the first place prize money of $20,000. I should in all honesty mention that after paying the entrance fee along with the additional extraordinary on-the-road expenses of food, ground transportation, countless tourist trophies and numerous admission costs, the $20,000 prize money would allow any-body who eventually won this first of it's kind global junket, to just about break even. Uncle Sam the Tax Man please take note!

Of greater significance to us than merely taking home the essentially kiss-your-sister prize money, was the actual adventure of having a blind date with the world. Our healthy egos were pushing us along on this uncharted journey because winning it would be proof in the pudding of Andy and I being exceptional world travelers. And in finally having the opportunity of confirming this romantic fantasy of ours in a straightforward, no-holds-barred competition with other equally aggressive travel savvy competitors. The truth from the very beginning was that we wouldn't get to keep any of the loot, even if we had won because we had a sponsor/investor. Our patron was a wealthy Beverly Hills industrialist. In addition to being a generous philanthropist and global adventurist-at-heart, he was also my good friend, Neil Breton, the savvy innovative Chairman and CEO of Breton Industries, a pri-vately-held LA-based conglomerate.

We gathered in *Baghdad-by-the-Bay* with the other eccentric bunch of racers, seventeen two-person teams in all, high atop the *Holiday Inn-Union Square*. Ever so cautiously, we were hovering some thirty-two stories up just ten short days after the *Loma Prieta* 7.1 earthquake had rock 'n' rolled the Bay Area's *World Series* between the A's and Giants. (*Do you remember where you were at 5:04 p.m. October 17th, 1989?*) Nervous? You bet!

This initial HumanRace briefing was Andy and I's first chance to size the other teams up, and believe me, plenty of experienced poker-face bluffing and audacious self-effacing posturing took place. Liars poker to be exact. Later, after the aforementioned liquid rules session, we met the media reps from both the print and network pencil corps, and devoured an impressively color-coded buffet table. Little did we know at the time that this bountiful feast was the HumanRace's version of the *Last Supper*. Finally, we met with the corporate sponsors of the event. They were major players with national and international brands to hawk for sure, but all of whom will go nameless here due to lack of contractual obligation!

Following a few friendly toasts of chilled Russian vodka, in anticipation of our triumph in the HumanRace, by some of the gracious patrons at *Tosca*, one of our favorite City haunts, we were escorted to San Francisco International Airport.

At the stroke of midnight, we boarded a *Singapore Airlines* 747 Big Top bound for China. It was to be a spine-numbing sixteen-and-a-half hour flight into the blackhole of the time-space continuum. We departed on Thursday and arrived on Saturday, losing Friday altogether, my personal favorite day of the week. I glumly accepted the fact that there would be no ritual *TGIF* bash and weekly debriefing session with my mates at *Chaya Venice* in Santa Monica. It was to be that kind of bizarre adventure; where whole days would just disappear in the heat of battle.

As we slipped the surly bounds of earth riding a vapor trail across that great intersection in the sky of the *International Date Line* and *Tropic of Cancer*, JB distributed to all the teams, in hermetically sealed envelopes, the list of scavenges for the first leg of the race. It was quite a catalog of interesting things to see and do in the Far East. We learned for the very first time just where the hell we were headed. There was no going back now.

Reading our scavenge list of the Southeast Asian leg, we discovered we would be going to/through: Hong Kong, Indonesia (Java and Bali), Malaysia (Along with the Island of Penang) along with Singapore, in no particular order. That was for us to determine, presumably through careful planning and scheduling. I know that I wasn't the only competitor who had never even heard of some of the more exotic destinations on that long list.

As the other teams quickly plotted and planned, studied and organized in guarded secrecy, Andy and I calmly ordered up another nightcap and sunk into our seats for a short nap. Not because we were overly optimistic or confident by any means, but, after looking over the scavenger list, we both figured that this may indeed be our last chance to sleep for some time to come...

Changes in Latitude=Changes in Attitude

You really come alive, probably because you feel so close to death, when you descend from the heavens after a tediously long trans-Pacific flight on your final approach into *Kai Tak International Airport* in Hong Kong. It's a real treat. For the first time visitor it's definitely a white knuckle experience. A *Disneyland E-ticket* ride to be sure. God help the poor soul that awakens on the final approach with groggy eyes and gazes out the window. The airplane's protruding wings pass but inches from the surrounding balconies of the ten-to-fifteen story apartment buildings lining the city-center runway. For a surrealistic and fleeting nanosecond you feel like a Peeping Tom. You're so close that laundry hanging on the balconies gets blow-dried in the wake of the jet's exhaust. Come to think of it, knowing how industrious the folks of Hong Kong are, maybe it is indeed a commercial dry cleaning operation *au naturale?* Anyway, you really get that nauseating feeling that you're going to splatter, as they say in flight attendant-speak. It seems like you're actually going to crash into one of these tall blocks of cement and steel and meet with a gruesome, premature and altogether untimely death. You find yourself whimpering the name of your mother and invoking other sacred deities. Your life flashes before you in a quick montage of snippets like an MTV video, as you simultaneously hear, then feel, the fuselage rattling accompanied by the unnerving whoosh of hydraulic fluid as the wheels are locked into position prior to an euphoric touchdown. And then the frightening thump of contact with *terra firma* followed by the screaming of the tires on the blackened tarmac.

As you're slowing and being brought closer to the safety of the terminal, you feel like yelling, "Oh, thank you mother!"

"Ladies and gentlemen welcome to Hong Kong," the flight's purser intones over the cabin intercom, "we hope that you've enjoyed your flight and please fly with us again real soon." For a quick moment you think you can detect a mocking tone in the voice. "Yea, right!" you mutter as you try clearing that potato-sized lump from your throat and wipe the flop sweat from your furrowed brow, "as soon as I dig this seat cushion out from underneath my fingernails!" You begin to wonder if this is just a precursor to having bamboo inserted under your fingernails. Now I'm no Hong Kong neophyte. Even old China hands hate this final approach. And to think in typhoon season it gets even trickier...

Take this flight, get a window seat on the right side if you dare! Have a few stiff drinks prior to landing and tell me I'm wrong. I dare you. No, I double dare you. Some great traveling sage was right when he suggested in his utter disdain for airline travel; that everybody indeed is a hostage once the jet takes off. This flight is proof of it. It's sheer torture in length and ending.

Hong Kong, our initial Human*Race* destination, was a distinct blur. Distinct in the fact that we were once again visiting what is frequently hailed as the *Pearl of the Orient*. It's a city of infinite contradictions to me. An incomparable jam-packed port city, home to a commercially energetic six million plus people where East confronts, no it collides, into the West. Where ultra-modernistic 21st Century technological realities come face-to-face with ancient time-honored spiritual traditions. A place where extravagant displays of opulent wealth and unrestrained consumption sit alongside widespread deprivation and generational poverty.

Hong Kong, is like, well, *Hong Kong*. It's one of a kind. But, Hong Kong also proved to be a visually frightening blur as our stay in this high-charged floating metropolis, a nation-state synonymous with fast cash, exotic cuisine (13,000 plus restaurants!), financial mega-deals, global trading, high-tech cellular phones and 24-hour custom made suits, lasted for a grand total of six and a half hours! It was to be a virtual sojourn in comparison with some of our other global municipal tours.

In 1997 the Brits will be officially leaving their last colonial outpost in Southeast Asia and the locals are a bit nervous with the inevitable Red Chinese takeover. The sun will indeed officially set on the British Empire on June 30th, 1997. Vancouver, Canada and Sydney, Australia seem to be the desired exile hot spots. Mandarin restaurants and residential property values are booming in both those cities. But nervous Hong Kongers are buying any passport they can get their hands on. Many have even plucked down HK$5,000 to purchase a passport for the sandy beached but wholly fictitious nation of *Corterra* whose handsome and slick brochure says is an "…official South Pacific nation." Yea sure…and I've got a…But hey, it looks official anyway.

We had luxurious accommodations awaiting us in ever-vibrant Hong Kong at the *Holiday Inn-Golden Mile* located along the Nathan Road shopping district on the Kowloon side. Unfortunately, we were only able to visit the hotel during two frenzied non-stop "*Hi, how'ya doin*?" passes through its terminally busy lobby. Dodging the international media milling about covering the event took some effort on our part. We visited our suite once for a quick hosing down in the art-deco black and pink shower. This was followed by an even quicker collection of our bags en route to the airport six hours later. We did have time however, to empty the mini-bar of all its liquid contents, and for this we give the friendly-staffed hotel our warmest regards along with a respectable three-star Chalmers-Valvur hotel mini-bar rating. Moreover, my personal, ever expanding hotel soap collection just wouldn't have been complete without their worthy representation.

Anonymous Travel Collections…
ashtrays
barf bags
foreign currency

miniature alcohol bottles
lovers
maps
refrigerator magnets
restaurant & bar matches
miniature spoons
pilot wings
airline playing cards
postcards
hotel bath robes
shot glasses
hotel soap
stamps
coins
hotel stationary
swizzle sticks
destination T-shirts
hotel towels
travel stickers
tickets stubs

We utilized our time rather efficiently in Hong Kong. We had theorized on the plane, that we could probably tend to all our assigned scavenges in approximately four fast-paced hours and still have time to catch the late afternoon plane departing Hong Kong for a remote island destination called Penang in Malaysia. As a result, our memories of this splendid South China Sea port city are blurred by the velocity at which we traveled through, around, up and then down it. We were sightseeing at sixty miles per hour.

Having no idea where some things were, we literally started from the top of our scavenger hunt list. Outside customs we hailed a cab and told him we needed to find the sacred and colorful *Wong Tai Sin*

Shinto Temple; from there it was a toss-up. Suddenly, we were in search of a global guidance counselor. Do we go across the harbor and take the scenic, near-vertical tram ride up to the unforgettable atmospheric panoramic heights of Victoria Peak, or do we take a trip on a standing-room-only train aboard the famously efficient *Kowloon-Canton Railway* in search of a lively rural market town named *Fan Ling* in the New Territories adjacent to the Communist border? We opted for *Fan Ling*. After that there were five other duties to perform in this mega-mall masquerading as a metropolis, and we expedited our assignments in a most fastidious manner. We went from using an abacus in *Fan Ling* to a laptop PC in Kowloon. We were fast. "As fast," as one expressive indigenous taxicab driver put it, "as the six million equity refugees will be scurrying to leave Hong Kong come July 1997, when the Brits finally hand over the keys of their once proud Imperial Colony to those bloody hot heads of Tiananmen Square massacre fame." I could only surmise that that was pretty damn fast!

After barely catching a *Star Ferry* across the perpetually busy sampan, luxury yacht, high speed hydrofoil and junk-filled Victoria harbor, followed by an excruciating, lung-burning quarter-mile mad dash through the congested Saturday afternoon streets of hot and humid Kowloon Peninsula to the airport, we settled comfortably into our seats on board the *Singapore Airlines* Mega-Top 747, albeit in row sixty-six, the last two seats available, while somehow averting an extremely unhealthy cardiovascular blowout with our frenzied pace.

We didn't have time to check up on our stock portfolios at Hong Kong's *Hang Seng* exchange. Didn't even have time to taste one of Hong Kong's mouth watering culinary specialties: shark-fin soup, tasty dim sum or sample the heavenly orange pancakes at the grand old dame of Southeast Asian hotels, the *Peninsula*, as we whisked past a group of black pajama-clad *tai chi* practitioners.

We did however, have a slight change in plans. We were now en route, not to Penang, Malaysia as our abbreviated strategic planning session had previously indicated, but to the city-state of Singapore. "Oh well…" I reassured Andy, "At least we're moving on right?" We had a fast start to nowhere. We were in the wake of an unseen object.

Round One of the Human*Race* was securely under our belts. Eighteen more to go! But we didn't know that at the time. It was for the best that we were kept in the dark about our many-more-to-follow destinations, we would later come to realize; for JB had many more tricks up his sleeve.

We arrived at Singapore's ultra-modern and highly efficient *Changi International Airport* around 10 p.m.. We immediately performed what would affectionately come to be known as the *airline schedule boogaloo*. Our tribal road dance. A logistical probing of transportation alternatives, schedules and theoretical angles in a continuous search for any advantage. Our particular division of labor had us each doing what we did best: Andy, (Now retired, by way of a golden parachute lest someone think he's really old, he's in his mid to late *thirtysomething*!) after a nine year misspent youth stint as a courteous and extremely capable *Pan Am* flight attendant, was charged with booking flights and checking out our vast array of global scheduling options. While I, being a trained international economist and practicing info-junkie, was charged with, what else, foreign currency exchanges, scrounging for high energy foodstuffs and finding any and all types of potentially vital tourist information. A copy of the local version of the *OAG* was always a prized find, as were regional maps and any and all open market satellite imagery photos.

"*Should we stay or should we go?*" to paraphrase *The Clash*, was the burning question of the moment. Being involved in a race, the question begged itself. A boisterous "Keep on moving!" became our continuous battle cry no matter how hungry or tired we were to become.

When you're continent-hopping, in a foreign environment, stressed out and suffering from extreme jet lag, you inevitably begin to hallucinate fantasy-based options. Like having a clean bed, room service, or a hot shower. Or indulging in an arousing and appetizing dinner for four maybe. Dancing even. But no, these were all but mirages of the mind. So keeping our blood sugar levels at an optimum thinking capacity proved to be extremely important during the course of the race. Clarity of thought, we believed, was crucial to our success, let alone our personal sanity and physical survival. The minimization of, what 17th Century military theorist Karl von Clausewitz called *friction*, was to be our entire Human*Race* mode of operation. Wasted down time is, well, just that, wasted time! At airports, train and bus stations, and other travel crossroads you've got to decide your fate quickly.

After not being able to talk our way onto the last flight to Penang despite promises of sexual favors, phone numbers of crooked immigration lawyers in LA and cold hard cash, we resigned ourselves to the fact that Kuala Lumpur was to be our next destination.

The locals refer to Kuala Lumpur simply as KL and it's in the very heart of the tropical Malaysian peninsula. A centrally located city from which we could take care of three other sets of scavenges.

Arriving dreadfully late at KL's *Subang International Airport* on board a virtually empty *Malaysian Airlines* DC-10, we proceeded directly to our prearranged hotel. With the knowledge that *Holiday Inn* was one of the Human*Race*'s main sponsors, it was with a certain air of confidence that we approached the no surprises *Holiday Inn-On-The-Park*, only to discover that, you guessed it, *surprise*, there were no more rooms at the inn. We were quickly advised that two things had stymied our now urgent room requests. First, we were informed, nay, actually chastised by the hotel's ill-mannered night manager, for being two full days ahead of schedule. "Schedule, what schedule?" Andy wondered aloud. "This was a race for chrissakes!" "You should be alerting the nobles of the local media of our arrival in KL and get some free publicity," I suggested to the wholly uninterested hotel manager. Nothing doing. Then the manager drops the big bomb on us. Due to a high-level *Commonwealth Heads of Government Meeting* (CHOGM) road show visiting town (The locals cynically, yet aptly referred to it as the Cheap Holiday on Government Money!) there were no rooms available for us common Commonwealth citizens.

I quickly informed the nasty night manager that I grew up in Canada, a Commonwealth nation, and that I had even studied in England, the most common of Commonwealth countries. Still nothing. We gave up trying to force our way in. Bribery clearly wasn't gonna work with this guy, and there were way too many short stocky guys promenading about the marble floored lobby in blue blazers, mirrored sunglasses and wires running into their ears. Headphones I thought. Secret Service? Terminators? Maybe…Jet lagged, running without the benefit of sleep for over 34 hours now, we backed off. Too tired to make a scene, but too wired to stay.

While we were being briskly escorted from the lobby, I told Andy that I wasn't about to bed down in the same hotel as the wicked-witch-of-the-rich Maggie Thatcher on ideological grounds alone. Let alone the fear of IRA hitmen! Nor would I share the hardwood floor with India's Prime Minister Rajiv Gandhi, he's no Mohandes Gandhi! As for all-around-nasty *apartheid*-supporting Pik' Botha of South Africa, well, we both agreed that he could be shown the nearest door and rightly deserved to snooze out in the cold with the dogs and flies. After all, we had our pride you know.

We eventually called on the *Ming Court Hotel*, popular with the younger KL execs and not on the list of approved accommodations for the heads of Commonwealth countries apparently. We set up our own incarnation of the good Doctor Hunter S. Thompson's international affairs suite for the night. The older of us, Andy, didn't remember any of this in the morning because he was beyond tired and looking for a new definition for exhaustion. Yes, he was drooling with fatigue when I pushed him onto his bed.

Included in the price of the suite was a decorative arrow in the corner of our room pointing in the direction of Mecca, Islam's holiest place, so we could pray, if we so desired, in the appropriate sanctified direction. "You need that," I sarcastically muttered to Andy, "When you're considering a conversion of religions on the road, it's those little extra special amenities that tip the balance."

We mapped out our ground incursion strategy of the Malaysian Peninsula before quickly dozing off, well before we could finish off our first beers of the day.

"Wouldn't you just know it," Andy yelled the next morning, "we missed out on Bob Hope's gala extravaganza at the KL *Hilton* last night. Oh well, guess we'll have to wait for his annual Christmas show with the troops." And the way I was now reading the Pentagon and State Department's recent smoke signals, this year's celebrity road show was probably gonna be held in Panama City! (Note: This chronicle was written between mid-December 1989 and January 1990. Now I'd have to say Bob Hope's 1990 Christmas extravaganza will be held *somewhere* in the Saudi Arabian desert, south of Kuwait. No, make that, er, well you choose: Bosnia, Somalia, Sudan, Rwanda, etc...)

A fine Muslim gentleman named Mustifa along with his overly inquisitive pimple-faced teenage son, Ismil, whom we'd met on the night flight into KL, offered us some sensible recommendations as to how to best handle our Malaysian itinerary. In fact, he offered us a ride, along with his family, to the seaside town of Malacca, our pending destination the next day. However, ethical issues arose between Andy and I out of his generous offer. After consulting with our crack roving Legal Department, which consisted of Andy's overwrought conscience and my highly pragmatist thinking honed on the playing fields of Eton, and after putting the sensitive, but in my humble opinion non-issue, to a secret, smoky boardroom-type of vote that ended in a deadlock, Mustifa's generous and friendly invitation was respectfully declined. The *Marquess of Queensberry* rules didn't apply to the HumanRace.

Although JB's rules of engagement on this trip were vague on such issues, private versus public transportation, we ultimately concurred that it might have violated the true spirit of the race by accepting the gracious offer. And as much as we wanted to do things as quick as humanly possible during this race, and this ride would have saved us several hours of valuable time, we conducted ourselves in what we felt was the underlying spirit of the Human*Race*. Later however, much to our chagrin, we discovered after a UN General Assembly-like meeting in Indonesia with all the other contestants, that this type of alternative transportation, hitchhiking along with rides in private cars and the like, were well within the spirit of the race, as well as within the legal guidelines of the race. Indeed, it was the very point of the Human*Race*, as I adamantly extolled to the crowd, to enable contestants to interact with different cultures and people up-close and personal.

Despite the secret ballots, it was later reported by an *ABC NEWS/Washington Post* exit poll that the voting went along party lines, Chalmers-yes and Valvur-no.

Many of these so-called gray areas between what's right and what's wrong arose during our frenzied dash around the world, and on each and every occasion the two of us anguished over just what to do. Situational ethics can be a real bitch in the heat of battle. However, between us we seem to have the suitable combination of reformed sinner and lapsed saint personalities, to deal with any and all of the moral dilemmas confronting us. The event we were engaged in, was in fact the first of it's kind ever attempted. We had no standardized "*Roberts Rules of Order*" to follow. The logistical problems faced by JB and his highly capable entourage were utterly staggering in both scope and dimension. Just think about it, thirty-four highly-competitive and varied individuals racing around the world, going from city to city and country to country in a matter of a couple of weeks. Needless to say, human nature being what it is, many squares were circled, along with numerous i's not dotted and t's not crossed properly. In many cases, the rules were made up as we traveled.

We covered KL, Malacca and Penang during the next twenty-four hours, despite the inconvenience of traveling through a country in the throes of an obscure and highly immobilizing religious holiday weekend called *Deepavali*.

Celebrated every November, *Deepavali* is a sacred Hindu holiday, also known as the Festival of the Lights that celebrates *Rama's* victory over the demon-King *Ravana*. Despite our crash course in local religious mythology, we stayed our course and pushed slowly ahead. This included an over-night train ride through the dense 150-million-year-old Malaysian Peninsula rainforest to the coastal town of Butterworth. You can tell that the British have been here! Not only because of some of the clearly out-of-place Anglo-Saxon town names...Butterworth? In Southeast Asia! Just who do they think they are anyway? But also because of the extensive regional communication system and amazingly efficient railway transportation network. The latter built by the British Army's SAS troops to aid their long-standing quarrel against the then Malay Communist insurgency.

The Malay people are stunningly beautiful, charitable and extremely friendly. They offered us assistance or a smile at every turn. *Selamat pagi* (Good day!) and *Apa khabar* (How are you?) were heard over and over again as we strolled the dusty streets. There are some seventeen million citizens in this emerging democracy. It is an incomparable ethnic and religious mix of diverse peoples: the Malay, Islamic peoples are the majority; the Chinese, Buddhists and Confucius's are the largest minority; with large factions of Indians, both Hindu and Sikhs, and European Christians and Jews. Actually, Malaysia is a uniquely constructed constitutional monarchy, made up of thirteen states, of which nine are administered by feudal hereditary rulers, all sultans, with a nominal rubber-stamp parliament seated in the capital city of Kuala Lumpur. The *Yang di-Pertuan*, or King of Malaysia, sits on his blue velvet and golden throne in downtown KL.

The Malaysian economy is currently one of the strongest in Southern Asia, with the fastest GNP growth rate in its geographic area. And rightly so. With over seventy-five percent of the country covered by lush dense tropical rainforests, natural resources are bountiful and harvested in an increasingly progressive way according to the Minister of Natural Resources. Or so they claim! Tin, cocoa, rubber and palm oil plantations are everywhere. Malaysia is also awash in a sea of underground oil reserves to boot. This country definitely has a promising economic. It has that prosperous jungle-frontier feeling to it. Now I'm not a licensed broker or anything remotely as sinister, although junkbond king Michael Milken's office keeps calling for advice (SEC please note that I haven't returned any of his bothersome business calls!) but...I strongly recommend that you buy into the *Malaysian Fund* (MF-NYSE), while you can afford it. Remember you heard it here first.

Prior to taking what would become our first encounter with truly public transportation, a bus filled with live clucking chickens, the smell of the catch-of-the-day, giggling kids and a lot of people just plain staring at us, we took care of several minor scavenges in KL. Elapsed time..? About an hour! KL, literally translated means Muddy Estuary and is a colorful city of about a million people mixing old and new and surging rapidly towards the eve of the 21st Century. Gleaming modern high-rises, busy broad boulevards, top-notch hotels, fast food eateries, government buildings, sports stadiums, sprawling factories, and a wide variety of temples, pagodas and mosques, all make KL a difficult city to pigeon hole.

Meanwhile back at the race...we ran into a couple of fellow racers whom we'd dubbed the Del Ray Boys at one of the markets. Rumors had already started to fly thick and fast, or was it hot and heavy? Anyway, some people had us already in Bali far ahead of the pack. Other rumors told of cheating and whole scale forging of scavenges. Humans and money. It was rapidly turning into some odd unedited version of "*It's a Mad, Mad, Mad, Mad World!*"

Somehow inspired by the other HumanRacers confidence in us, we quickly visited the magnificent Moorish-designed local railway station. Constructed in 1911, it mixes beautifully with the turn-of-the-century

Northern Indian style. Then it was off to nearby *Masjid Jame* (Jame Mosque). Finally, we called on KL's somewhat neo-traditional craftwork shopping center. A typical Southern California swap meet this was not. Then it was to the back of the bus for a trek through the countryside.

It was in Malaysia's version of canal-ridden Venice, the famous port town of Malacca, also known as *Melaka*, that we encountered the historic vestiges, the distinct architecture and extensively varied cuisine of several colonial powers rise and fall from geopolitical grace. A town of about half a million people, it seems to have been the jewel of many a leader's eyes, due, no doubt, to its historically strategic position as an important Southeast Asian port and trading center.

A brief but illustrious history lesson goes something like this: First came the famous lost Hindu fishermen. Seeing the seductive figures of the local women, they happily immigrated, trading in their ships for poles. In 1405, the famous Chinese Admiral Cheng Ho arrived and allowed his ethnic traders to expand their commercial markets. Even then we can see how vitally important market share was as an accepted business concept. He quickly pissed-off the encroaching Siamese army, loose on an ornery binge, and then allowed the overly zealous and extremely righteous proselytizing Islamic hordes into the region. Business is business I guess! Since the early 1500's, the seemingly always accommodating Malaysians have been visited by the colonial-minded Portuguese, replaced by the equally colonial-minded Dutch in 1641 following a long and bitter siege, and then by the irrepressible *British East India Company* under the tutelage of a snobbish British Captain named Francis Light, in 1786. More recently, though ever so briefly, the Malaysians were victimized by the militant *Land of The Rising Sun* Japanese running amok in Southeast Asia. And after a brief diplomatic squabble with the British Imperialists following World War II, the Malay people have been wholly independent since 1957. In a nutshell, a checkered but much celebrated road to independence, or *merdeka* as they say here.

Although we only stayed in Malacca for about three hours, it was an intense three hours of Q & A and sightseeing. Relics of by-gone eras were our destinations: the massive pink colored Dutch townhall known as *Stadthuys*; the Portuguese built *Saint Paul's Church* and the *Porta de Santiago* fortress; the oldest Chinese temple in Malaysia called *Cheng Hoon Teng Temple*; and finally, a visit to the old part of Malacca, now supplanted with ship pirates, Chinese junkbond salesman, Shiite arms dealers, Japanese tourists and Polish-run hamburger joints selling ice cold *Diet Cokes*.

One of the more interesting scavenges aside from photographing yet another colonial relic was to find the last guy in the world who makes shoes for older Chinese women who've had their feet bound, and buy a pair. No shit. This guy isn't exactly as busy as *Footlocker* but when your feet are size 4 inches he's the only game in town. Town, hell! He's the only game in Asia! Talk about a dying breed. His shoes, made of brocade, and very dainty and beautiful, completely belie the ugly reality of what they're for.

Malacca's cousin coastal island-city of Georgetown (Yep, the British have been here too!) located on the beautiful Island of *Pinang* (Penang) to the far north was even more diverse. It's an easygoing, yet cosmopolitan resort area where rickshaws are the most popular and widespread mode of transportation. Here we visited in a *post-haste* manner two particularly tranquil and sacred places.

But I tell the story too quickly…By the time we got our bags out of the hotel, and ran to the station, in the middle of one of those torrential downpours you only get in countries with *bona fide* rainforests, it had been many hours since we'd last eaten. I stood in line to get our train tickets, while Andy shot some B-roll video footage. With about an hour to spare before our departure, we needed to eat. I can always tell when Andy needs to eat because he starts snapping at me. Or we start snapping at each other. Whatever. Who's fault it is, is not important here. Food is! Andy knew of a place where we could get a good steak

(Yes, Andy had spent a New Year's Eve here once.) but it was a taxi ride away and we were so punchy from lack of nutrients, jet lag and general hurly burly that we just snapped at each other.

That accomplished, we strode over to a nearby *A & W* across from the train station for a burger. I swore Andy to secrecy on this, but it's too funny not to tell. Here we are in Kuala Lumpur, easily one of the more exotic cities in the world and we're at an *A & W* scarfing down double-bacon cheeseburgers and rootbeer floats. Food in motion. In all fairness, it was the nicest, most efficient *A & W* I'd ever been in. It even had a doorman and a *maitre'd*. You gotta love countries with a large labor pool. I got the feeling that the employees thought that they were being put to the test by us. We were, after all, Americans and as such, used to the real thing. We smiled a lot, and they even opened the doors for us on the way out. I'd like to see that happen at an LA *A & W*!

We were now living out a traveler's dilemma of sorts: KL, as I've already borne witness to, is an intriguing sophisticated world-class city especially known for its diverse selection of eating establishments. We had unrestricted expense accounts but a highly restrictive schedule. As a result, instead of dinning in some three-star *Michelin* restaurant, we found ourselves scarfing down cheeseburgers, fries and rootbeer floats! An ugly memory induced by an extremely low blood/sugar level. We had reluctantly succumbed to foraging for fast food in a gross attempt at carbo and calorie packing. It was a trans-global junk food chain pit stop.

Clearly, the world is changing dramatically by the year, month, day, hour and micro-second. Nowhere on the face of this blue planet can a fast food outlet not be found, by anyone skilled enough in looking for one. Hell, the basic skills involved in foraging for food have changed. After all, we've evolved too, we're not hunters and gatherers anymore. We're now just petty consumers. We ate with a certain degree of humility.

Fully sated, we boarded the night train, confident in our standing in the race. We were just tearing up the Asian countryside. Then again, reality intrudes. On board were the Del Ray Boys hot on our tail, headed north with us. We swallowed a handful of sleeping pills and passed out.

Wat Chayamangkalarm, a Thai-style Buddhist temple that houses, at 32-meters long, what's reputed to be the "third largest reclining Buddha in the world," was our first Penang destination. What an alluring claim-to-fame and marquee billing we thought. Think about it, *third* biggest mall in the world, or *third* longest suspension bridge in the world, or better yet, seeing the *third* largest Liberty Bell replica in the world.

Our other destination, *Kek Lok Si Temple*, is an extensive spiritual compound located on the lush, Kelly-green bluffs that overlook this historic harbor town. *Kek Lok Si* is a harmonious blend of rather unique and distinct looking Chinese, Thai and Burmese architectural elements. It is an utterly fascinating place where we witnessed the sacrificial burning of joss sticks as we sought out the answers to our more worldly clues. The so-called *Ten Thousand Buddha's Pagoda* surrounded by souvenir stalls, lurking turtles and fish ponds was our desired destination. The directions, upon entering this massive Buddhist temple were: "Up the stairs, past the burning joss sticks, left at the turtle pond, past the begging-bowl laden monks, past the Goddess of Mercy, right at the Emerald Buddha and you're there." Took us ten minutes.

It was also while traipsing across the island of Penang that we encountered one of our more unforgettable and heart-warming experiences during the entire Human*Race*.

While en route to the cloudy summit of Penang Hill, a cool two-thousand foot plateau that on a clear day affords you a breath-taking three hundred and sixty degree view of the entire island, we came across a friendly and extremely lively, congregation of local school kids out on a field trip. We cut the tremendously long queue using our satellite feed to America scheme.

At this point I should let you in on a few of our more noteworthy travel tricks. We readily employed our wild imaginations along the way, and engaged a wide variety of scams in the hope of expediting and/or facilitating our quick and safe passage through rather untimely and/or potentially sticky situations. Along with the relatively mundane satellite feed to America idea, we were at various times performing a congressional fact-finding mission, or pretending to be officials of the *International Association of Tour Operators* conducting a global tourism survey. We also purported to be *CNN News* correspondents, an *MTV* film crew or money-laden venture capitalists scouting out Third World investment opportunities. And when the mood struck, or the unfamiliar occasion called, we transformed ourselves into well-cultivated wayfaring English gentlemen. The one that got us the most bang-for-the-buck, as it were, was of course the good old Hollywood producer/location scout angle. This particular scam, popular in the LA area too, had us scouting out various movie locations and casting locals for the up 'n' coming "*Rambo: Part IV*" mayhem and gratuitous violence epic. On a few occasions we wondered if calling in an anonymous bomb scare to the airlines was legal if we were close to missing our plane's departure time? (*FBI, CIA, INTERPOL, RCMP, MI-5, NSA, DEA, LAPD, OPP, MOSSAD, CSIS, KGB and FAA, among dozens of other secret international agencies, please take note this is only a joke! Okay, a bad joke I admit it! Honest guys, it's just a joke…really!*)

At any rate, at the foot of Penang Hill we crammed on board a tram with about seventy extremely polite and giggling youngsters for a bumpy thirty minute funicular railway journey to the top. Andy, I had previously learned while in Rio de Janeiro en route to the top of famed Sugarloaf Mountain, is somewhat leery of all cable car rides. Not the rides themselves mind you, but the structural integrity of Third World-built sites. And just as he was climbing Victoria Peak in Hong Kong yesterday, here too he was a tad nervous about the crowded conditions of the tram ride until I noticed that it was designed and built by the Swiss. After quickly pointing this out to him in a sincere effort to calm his fears, I reminded him matter-of-factly, "…that you can always trust the Swiss!" Somewhat relieved by this highly respected engineering badge of distinction, he relented to the task at hand. I never mentioned the lowest bidder issue...

Andy then proceeded to pull out all the stops in trying to entertain this tough captive audience with his finely tuned comedy routine crafted in the seedy nightclubs of San Francisco, LA and New York City. Talk about a tough crowd! Being a political comic, Andy lampoons politicians. What do these kids know about Oliver North or Dan Quayle? He ended up a song and dance man, singing old *Beatles* tunes. Believe me when I say that any white guy singing anything that resembles a rock song would have been a hit.

By the time we arrived at the top of beautiful Penang Hill, Andy had the entire group, including their overly protective and anal teachers, laughing and singing in unison some of their favorite old *Top 40* songs. We also heard six passionately sung courses of the Malay national anthem. Of course to see the exclusive comedy stylings of Andy entertaining the troops with his unique array of high comedy skits and sketches, you'll just have to go over to his house for the limited engagement, private screening of some of our twenty-two odd hours worth of semi-riveting, uncut Human*Race* travel videos. And you thought Andy Warhol's "*Sleep*" was a long movie. Well, suffice it to say, we saved these unforgettable pieces of time, our time, on the Human*Race* as visual mementos for prosperity. You won't see any of this spectacularly rare footage on an *HBO "Comedy Special"* or even the *Travel Channel.* Let's just say film at eleven folks!

Departing this peaceful area of Northern Malaysia from Penang's *Bayan Lepas International Airport,* on board a *Malaysian Airlines* Boeing-737, we stopped off in KL ever so briefly to hire a share taxi for the rest of our journey into the city-state of Singapore.

But again I skipped a few details...So we *did* the island of Penang from sunrise, when our train arrived, till about 11:30 a.m. It was our intention to be on a noon flight back to KL. Anyway, after our last stop at a temple that featured live snakes, we made a mad dash to the airport for the flight. We made it in seconds flat to no avail. The plane was full, except for two seats! But we were told we needed to have our tickets written for the next flight. "What's the difference? Can't we get on this one?" I wailed. No dice, they curtly replied. Paperwork is important. Then it hit me again...of course, the British had been here too. Their legacy? Correct paperwork. In triplicate. While this was being handled we took up station at the open air bar. Andy in his *San Francisco Giants* hat and me looking like *Indiana Jones'* evil twin. On one of my many forays to the loo through the airport I managed to latch on to a young British lass of indeterminate age. I figured twenty tops! She was on vacation with mummy and daddy and waiting to board their plane back to London. She was glad to escape from parental supervision for a while and hang out with "these two really scraggly and odd blokes full of weird tales..." Dad was equally concerned as he showed up promptly and raised an eyebrow over his daughter's tossing back a few lagers with these...these...hoodlums. I of course, being a former *London School of Economics* diplomacy student, quickly stepped in before Andy could slur anything offensive and allayed his fears about who his daughter was cavorting with. A formal introduction was made. We were, he decided upon further scrutiny, well educated if a bit road worn. His daughter, on the other hand, will prove to be a handful and is probably at this writing, riding on the back of a *Harley* chopper somewhere in Spain or San Bernardino with a guy named Butch sporting a tattoo or two. Ah the joys of fatherhood...

During our journey south we had taken it upon ourselves to guzzle untold quantities of local *Tiger Beer*. The bumpy five hour tour of mostly uncharted regions allowed us a chance to catch our breaths and unwind a bit. The cold beers went down oh so easily, and our progressively inebriated state allowed us to look back on the first few frenzied days of the race in utter giddiness. It had clearly been a manic 48 hours, and no less manic now as we took in the Malaysian scenery at eighty miles-per-hour. We were clearly losing track of time. And I mean days, not hours…"Looks a lot like Jersey!" is about all I can remember either one of us saying along the way. A sad commentary indeed.

Aside from the odd logging truck passing by, we didn't witness any massive deforestation projects ourselves during our trek through the Malaysian Peninsula's famous Penan Rain Forest, itself a large portion of the world's fragile life support system. It is apparently being cut down at an incredible one thousand acre-a-day clip by greedy Japanese timber conglomerates. Done, we're told, to supply lumber for massive Australian housing projects and to continue the endless replenishment of disposable wooden chop-sticks and toothpicks. What they need here is to establish a local chapter of the ideologically correct, yet controversially radical in their guerrilla-like actions, *Earth First!* eco-police battalion. I still remember one of my old mentors, Congressman Phil Burton's, famous environmental lines, "Terrorize the corporate bastards!" The inherent beauty and majesty of this place was obvious and ought to be preserved for eternity. I wondered if there were any gray spotted owls in them there hills?

This wild and wacky race around the world, no matter how superficial in the grand scheme of things, gave us a personal opportunity to fully comprehend the rapidly changing nature of our global village and the ultimate inter-dependency of all of its precious resources. As fast as we were traveling around the world, so too can revolutionary ideas be globally broadcasted, deadly diseases transmitted, along with the ultimate global solutions to everybody's uniquely local problems. These quick observations were not entirely lost on our weary and numbed brains.

Sometime after dark, we quickly passed through the Tijuana of Malaysia, Johore Bahru, the gateway to fabulous Singapore. We said our good byes to our fellow share-taxi lessees in the middle of a poorly lit, bustling market place area. We successfully bartered for a taxi across the Straits of Johore's severely congested causeway and got our passports stamped. Eventually we arrived, after a five hour drive to our delightful

Singapore destination, only a tad worse for the wear and drunker than two sailors on payday!

Singapore, the *Lion City*, sometimes also referred to as the Houston of Asia, is the second cutest little police state in the whole world. Switzerland is first, hands down, no competition! They never actually tell you what to do here, or in Switzerland for that matter, but somehow you constantly end up doing their will anyway. It's *Disneyland* with a death penalty! Their commander-in-chief, the benevolent dictator Prime Minister Lee Kuan Yew, has been in charge of the city-state's rather prosperous treasury since 1959. He seems harder to get rid of than an incumbent unindicted Southern Congressmen. Politically speaking, sources say that Mr. Prime Minister is to the right of Attila the Hun. Order and stability at any price, upheld by the commercial holy trinity of trade, banking and cheap labor, seems to be his main preoccupation in seeing that his Flying Tiger economic miracle sustains itself.

In the early seventies they'd go so far as to crop your hair on arrival if it was summarily judged too long or untidy by their strict authoritarian hygiene standards. Talk about your fashion police! Singapore is so immaculately clean that today it'll cost you five hundred dollars to spit on the street. Canning is an all too real social engineering tool. You have to *voluntarily* attend counseling sessions for the offense of littering. LA, *Litterers Anonymous*, has a big following here. Shock therapy is sure to follow for jaywalking. Singapore is so anal-retentive, it actually charges chronic non-flushers up to five hundred dollars for violating their strict "failing to flush" toilet laws. To date, over a hundred offenders have been charged! What I want to know is, how do they investigate this particular offensive offense? Does someone actually file a report?

Singapore's nasty and puritanical cultural police were more vindictive. They were men on a mission to be sure. They rid this now sterile city-state of not just *XXX*-rated movie houses, but banned *R*-rated movies as well from showing. It's definitely a *PG* country! Jukeboxes were even outlawed. Scandalously famous *Bugis Street*, on par with internationally renown *Bourbon Street* in New Orleans or *Place Pigalle* in Paris, was unceremoniously bulldozed into a heap of firewood. A carnival no more. Any and all forms of debauchery proved to be taboo in Singapore. Needless to say, the local opium dens, bawdy houses and rowdy dusk-to-dawn R & R fun zones were quickly sanitized and swept under the rug. Fun was expensive in Singapore these days, the cost of a plane ticket to Bangkok!

The eager, well trained and highly motivated workforce, all seem to comply with the so-called *3-S Productivity Plan*. Posted in every one of our spotless taxis, it requires the following of all employees:

1) Social Responsibility (Which means don't lie, cheat or steal.)

2) Service Attitude (Say 'yes sir' and 'yes madam' a lot.)

3) Skill (Give the illusion to the tourists that you know what you're doing.)

This once-upon-a-time backwater of a swampy fishing village was founded around 1100 AD by a Sumatran prince. Later, in the early 1800's, it was brought out of its frontier-like pirate town mentality by the now famous Sir Thomas Stamford Raffles of *Raffles Hotel* fame. (Closed at the time for a $90 million dollar renovation.) It eventually achieved total independence from both Malaysia and Britain in August 1965.

This sophisticated, modern, tidy, efficiently run mini-state, that Sigmund Freud would surely have diagnosed as suffering from a severe case of the dreaded *Napoleon Complex*, gives you a definite sense of instant Asia. Singapore has surpassed Hong Kong as the center of commerce in Southeast Asia due to two prominent factors: jet age transportation and global communications, and a strict, almost religious adherence to bullish free market principles. An amalgam of several cultures, Singapore's two and-a-half million industrious residents are the ultimate capitalists. Global trade, world-wide trans-shipping and international high finance are its three main lines of defense against the chronic economic underdevelopment that seems to plague so many non-Western Third World nations. Everything is for sale, and on sale here. And I mean everything!

But we weren't in a shopping frame of mind during our abbreviated stopover, for the contest was progressing and we were pushing the envelope a little bit further by the hour.

We did Singapore, amid the sweltering heat as befits its location, a scant inconsequential 1 degree north of the Equator, in our customary full tilt businesslike manner, four hours flat! This included side trips through many shophouses along Chinatown's convoluted and narrow alley ways adjacent to *Trengannu Street*, as well as a mini-tour through the much celebrated Little India neighborhood along *Serangoon Road*. We also happened to wander through *Arab Street*; the very center of Singapore's Muslim quarter. The exotic tastes, smells, and sights of these three distinct areas within walking distance of each other is beyond simple comparison. We were nearing cultural overdose. We also ventured a look-see into the bizarre *Bright Hill Buddhist Temple*. This is where, in full ceremony, they incinerate the faithful and stock-pile their charred remains (Inside a massive gymnasium-sized warehouse. The cremated ash remains are then deposited.) in small mustard colored urns, each adorned with an austere 2-by-3 black and white photograph of the deceased. Merely describing the foreboding feelings of unearthliness and eeriness doesn't do this place justice. It was like an out take from "*Soylent Green*." My neck hairs stood on end and a sense of claustrophobia engulfed us as thousands of dead eyes peered at us longingly. A throaty "out!" was continually muttered by Andy as the doorway out of this cavernous spiritual ash tray was quickly found.

After this spine-tinglingly morbid episode, Mr. Tang, our gracious and ever-enlightening taxicab driver while in Singapore, immediately got us back to our bright and airy hotel for a much needed little pick-me-up. We drank secure in the knowledge that we couldn't get out of town for several hours because of a flight connections bottleneck. There were only two flights a day that flew between Singapore and our next destination, Jakarta, Indonesia. So, we rewarded ourselves with some, unheard of up until this point, down-time. Yea, we got to do whatever we pleased for a whole three hours! What leisure. What freedom. What fun. *What to do?*

Usually, if I spend 24 hours or longer someplace, I do some basic recon to find out five things about the place I'm staying: 1) where's the best sunrise spot; 2) where's the best sunset spot; 3) where's a good place for a warm conversation and a cold beer; 4) where's the best local morning market; and finally, 5) where's the best restaurant in town. The *Five Essentials* I call them. But since we didn't have 24 hours to kill, we had other, more mundane ideas about how to pass our time productively.

So, tacky, scenic (With sights we'd never have time to actually see!) and envy inducing postcards were addressed. I regress here, but did you ever notice that you always get postcards from people long since out of your life? And they seem to rub their traveling laurels in, as if by saying via subliminal message on the postcard: "See, I'm a wonderful success and traveling the globe, and if you hadn't cruelly broken my heart, run away with my gay roommate and stayed with me, you would be here too!" No? Well okay, maybe not. But that's why I like to send them!

Laundry was done. Rolls of *Kodachrome* and batteries for the *Walkman* were procured. The *Indonesian Tourist Authority* was contacted for a little insider information as to our next destination. As usual, with so-called "tourist authorities," the well-intended nincompoops gave us inaccurate information.

We made telephone calls to the Motherland and loved ones, literary agents and investment brokers alike. (Yes…in that order. But I had checked the *Singapore Straits Times'* exchange index, and didn't like what I was seeing.) Finally, a few days worth of English newspapers were amassed. We also conducted a brief shopping safari along Singapore's hip, though ridiculously expensive and commercial *Orchard Road* area and finished with dinner at the world renown *Newton Circus* food emporium galleria extraordinaire.

Open 24/7, if it has to do with food, you can get it here. Lobster, pork rinds, exotic fruits, Mexican beers, glass noodles, steamed vegetables that haven't even been scientifically classified yet, pig knuckles, eel, dog kebobs, horse meat steaks, fishhead curry, ostrich egg omelets, fried garlic crickets, monkey-on-a-stick, *profuto* rolls, dried stock fish, peanut oil fried beetles, pizza slices, and yes, their famous sweet and sour sheep eyes. I myself had a plate of curried shrimp over vegetable fried rice, and a bowl of an extremely hot n' spicy type of Oriental-Hungarian goulash. Needless to say, this was all washed down with vast quantities of ice cold German beer. You could say it was a smorgasbord to end all smorgasbords. It definitely puts both *Sizzler's* salad bar and the $1.99 lunch at the *Flamingo Hilton* in Vegas to shame.

After quickly perusing the various papers over dinner, we learned that during our absence from the domestic information wars: the *Giants* had lost to the *A's* in the much delayed Bay Bridge *World Series* of 1989; that Wall Street was in a bearish mood for some unknown reason; that President Bush still hadn't decided on anything of significance during his first nine months; that the Berlin Wall was still standing; that Nelson Mandela was still being incarcerated in a South African prison; that Ron and Nancy Reagan were off selling whatever was left of their souls to the Japanese; that Ultimate Commander Manual Noriega was still snubbing his nose at drug czar Bill Bennett and his boys at the DEA; and finally, that the Communist Party was still reigning supreme throughout Eastern Europe and the Soviet Union. As the French say: *Plus ca change, plus c'est le meme chose.* But then again, *shit happens too* as they also say along the Venice Beach strand. And soon it would...

It proved to be yet another exhausting and mentally draining day despite our brief R & R session, as we were still suffering from severe bouts of jet lag. I may have indeed been physically on SDS, *Singapore Daylight Savings* time, but I was functioning on LA metabolism time. And it must have been very late! Our bodies were a bundle of frazzled nerve endings. We eventually made our way back to Singapore's *Changi*

International Airport just in time to catch a *Garuda Airlines AirBus* 300 South across the equator to Jakarta, Indonesia.

I want to digress here again and talk about Singapore's lilac-hued *Changi* International airport. Rumor has it that they're petitioning for *8th Wonder of the World* status. This is not just another international airport. *Changi* is a monument built for the international business traveler that Singapore so wants to impress. And impress they do! It is said that some sixteen million pampered travelers pass through this hub yearly, and for good reason too. You can shop in one of over one hundred shops offering rock bottom, get-your-*VISA*-cards-out prices. Or rent a day room complete with a private bath to shower 'n shave, or nap following one of those grueling fifteen hour flights for a mere twenty bucks. They have a totally automated *Skytrain* people-mover that whisks you off to your required terminal. Called by the builders an *airtropolis* (aviation city), this $400 million addition offers literally every possible amenity one can imagine. After a public sauna and work out in the gymnasium, transit passengers can take a free two-hour guided tour of the city, catch a flick at a theater, drop off the kids at a supervised children's play area, visit a science and technology exhibit and still take care of a little business at the high-tech business center that rivals none. The only thing this ultra-modern airport doesn't do is lose your luggage. It's against the law here and violating baggage handlers and sky cap porters alike, are shot on the spot! The only activity that American travelers will have to do without is those up close and personal gang-interventions by the Hare Krishnas as you rush from one gate to another. And you never have to walk anywhere. As far as moving sidewalks go, if all of the ones at *Changi* were placed end to end you could conceivably ride from LA to New York.

I also love *Changi* in spite of it being named after the most notorious Japanese prison camp in Asia. One really fun activity, if your suffering from terminal boredom, is to go watch the folks walk off the *British Airways* jumbos. The old timers visibly flinch when the overly polite Singaporeans say, "Welcome to *Changi*." Old memories die hard I guess…

A Journey Without Maps

The hot and heavy pungent aroma of clove cigarettes fills the deepest recesses of your nasal passages the minute you step off the aircraft in Jakarta. You either love it or hate it, there's simply no middle ground on the *kretek* cigarette issue. This was our welcome to Indonesia, the backdrop for the boy-meets-girl-in-tropical-downpour-political-thriller "*The Year of Living Dangerously.*"

Speaking of living dangerously...We filed through the Swiss-contracted Indonesian Customs and Passport Control nervously eyeballing several prominently displayed posters. They listed the various customs and import regulations, you know, the laws of the land, that we were about to stress fracture. You have to hand it to the Asians, subtlety is not their strongest suit. The picture of a hooded man with his head in a noose, was especially poignant. It didn't say what the condemned man's particular infraction was, but the point was clearly brought home.

We were about to be guilty, more or less, of the following Indonesian social, cultural and political crimes:

Importing Chinese writing and herbal medicines.

Importing a short-wave radio receiver.

Importing pornographic literature, Playboy. (Just for the articles of course!)

Importing Medfly infested fruits and unauthorized vegetables.

Importing subversive political literature, well, maybe guilty, maybe not I thought.

Importing a video camera without the proper A-D345-90OLM permit.

Importing audio cassette recordings, very guilty!

And finally, we also knew that we were willfully and knowingly in direct violation of a handful of Indonesia's ridiculously arcane and strict *foreign currency laws*. As it was, you could only import roughly two hundred American dollars or *rupiah* equivalent of cash into Indonesia. Which would only be enough to cover a medium-size bar-bill at the airports bar.

So with confident, unflinching poker faces, we nodded a steadfast "No!" in unison to each and every question issued from the young dignified, though highly gullible, Customs Officer. Apparently the surveillance cameras trained on our attitudes were also victimized by our successful bluff. The officer-in-charge quickly stamped our passports with a loud thud and waved us through. "No problem, man," I whispered to Andy who was bug-eyed and wet with perspiration. We looked at each other with eyebrows raised and breathed a collective sigh of relief and quickly caught the first taxicab we thought mechanically sound enough for the hour long ride into the city.

Being the wise, intrepid traveler that I am, I walked over to the first car I see moving and say we're going into town. Andy casually mentions that everybody else seems to be getting into the regulation red and white cabs...over there. "No...no, we're not waiting in line! This will be fine," I declare with all the experience of a man who's never been to Jakarta. "But they have air conditioning!" Andy observes. "We'll be fine," I insisted. So in we pile. Then I glance back at our fellow passengers getting into neat little ding-free taxis while exhaust fumes mingle with my sweat and I begin to have second thoughts.

Not ten minutes from the airport, our driver leaves the main highway and takes off down a dark, deserted road heading for...well we didn't know and it made us nervous. It really looked like a set-up. I could see the headlines: "*The bodies of two unidentified American tourists found in a shallow grave on the outskirts of Jakarta.*" The fact that we were carrying enough cash to equal the GNP of several small towns did not escape me. There are so many poor people in Jakarta that they'd as soon kill us for the dirty sneakers on our feet. We got about two hundred yards down an unlit stretch of unpaved road and both of us insisted in no uncertain terms that he immediately get back to the paved highway. He smiled and said, "OK...just trying to take the back road and not pay toll." He probably was just trying to save a few *rupiahs*. Probably the sum of about eight cents. We told him we'd tip him big...just get back on the main highway! We finally made it to the hotel minutes behind the others from the plane who didn't seem to be sweating as much as we were...

Jakarta, even under a relatively peaceful and dramatically lit yellow-hued harvest moon, is a frightful, seething and unsettling megalopolis. It's mass urbanization gone amok. A teeming urban slum with tens of thousands of destitute squatters sleeping and living out generations on the streets. Their humble abodes were fashioned out of high-density plastic sheeting, rusted tin and wooden crates marked *Genuine Toyota Spare Parts* or *United Nations Development Agency*. This polyglot megalopolis almost makes Calcutta, India or Dhaka, Bangladesh and Lagos, Nigeria look like nice places to live. On my own highly subjective *Global Urban Survivability Index*, Jakarta, which lacks any semblance of either charm, scenic beauty or a positive quality of life, rates somewhat below hellhole status. In fact, if Jakarta was enrolled in the international sister city program, *Hell* might indeed be her evil twin sister city.

This Islamic Republic surprises most people when you mention its sheer population. Indonesia does in fact, have the fifth largest population base in the world, with in excess of one-hundred and eighty-seven million impoverished souls. I'm absolutely convinced though, that the indigenous census takers gave up on their mission long ago and threw away their enumerator boards, admitting defeat, when they confronted chaotic Jakarta. So who really knows how many folks actually live here. It's a lost cause to be sure. It is guesstimated by *World Bank* and *United Nations* computer simulations and advanced degree bean counters, that by the year 2000, Jakarta alone will have over twenty-five million residents!

It further shocks one's practical making-ends-meet sensibilities when you come to realize that the average annual income of these teeming millions amounts to less than six hundred dollars. That's less than two bucks a day! How people can maintain even a marginally basic material existence, let alone hope for a better life for their children in such relentlessly unfavorable living conditions, is beyond my limited grasp of reality. I can only shake my head in wonder. That old, yet seemingly apt cliché: *There but for the grace of God go I*...crept into the recesses of my consciousness ever so suddenly while taxiing into town. It really makes you wonder if that old conservative thinker, Hobbes, may have indeed been correct when he said that life for most of the world's people was to be, *nasty, brutish and short*...!

You can better empathize with, as well as objectively appreciate, the proportion and complexity of many of the Third World's unique problems, when you supplement your personal travel experiences by attempting to absorb all the history, relevant information, and statistics of their enduringly dire socioeconomic predicament. That is, take a statistical snapshot of the place. Unfortunately, in this frighteningly grim situation the more you know about Indonesia in general, and Jakarta in particular, the more disheartening it gets.

Jakarta, also known in Indonesia as *Ibu Kota*, or Mother City, it should seem obvious by now, is on the imminent verge of either anarchy or total collapse. Probably both! It's just a matter of time. It was a tedious, bumpy, dusty and disturbingly eye-opening drive to our safeguarded sanctuary at the *Hotel Indonesia*. A concrete megablock complex with an impregnable armed perimeter, located in the very center of this mess. En route, we waded far too deep into the toxic soup of rainwater, sewage, grease, oil, litter, dirty dish water, and other assorted pollutants. We passed a scenic collision of old and new: high-rises towering next to cardboard and corrugated metal hovels; diesel-powered eighteen wheelers leaving pedal-powered *becaks* (trishaws) choking in the dust and a few commercial *Development Coming Soon* signs next to ancient temples.

Jakarta does have a remarkable history attached to it that goes back thousands of years. Its modern history however starts, of course, when the first white Euromen, in the name of the *Dutch East India Company*, took over in the 1520's crushing the Islamic troops staking out the region. Although its true golden era was probably during the Buddhist and Hindu period stretching from the 8th to the 15th centuries. Following the Dutch's cue, the British reigned supreme for a while until moving north to Singapore to establish multinational trading giants and franchise outlets. They then returned it *do-si-do*. Then it was the Japanese occupation until Hiroshima refocused their attention a little closer to home. To the locals it must have been seen as a continuous game of Colonial musical chairs. Or as Pete Townshend of *The Who* sings, "…meet the new boss. Same as the old boss…" Independence was finally proclaimed by the central government of Indonesia in 1949.

Aside from the usual cases of sporadic violence including: cyclical political uprisings, far too numerous to mention ethnic skirmishes, an ongoing communist insurgency, a nasty little CIA-engineered military *coup* and counter-*coup* in 1965 (*Which may have saved the country, but took over 500,000 lives!*), and eternal widespread political and economic anarchy in the surrounding 26 ethnic provinces, Jakarta has nonetheless somehow maintained its firm control over the far reaching 13,000 island Indonesian archipelago, albeit with an iron fist.

Indonesia is basically a military oligarchy run by President-for-Life strong man. Which could vary in length according to the promotion schedule of lesser officers! Suharto and his army thugs since the 1965 *coup*, when he and his CIA patrons deposed the great nationalist hero Sukarno. A feudal society for the most part, that embraces over 300 different ethnic dialects, is now run by the new Colonial masters in the capital city of Jakarta. An interesting concept known as *Pancasila*, or the "Five Principles," is the basis for the country's civilized, though highly corrupt, rule.

One: Belief in "One Supreme God." The nearest we could figure, the "One Supreme God" was either Mohammed, Buddha, Krishna, or Jesus Christ. But as long as you believe in "One Supreme God," I guess you're okay.

Two: A "Just and Civilized Humanity." But of course...

Three: The "Unity of Indonesia." Through the old divide and rule axiom...

Four: "Democracy revealed through respect and open dialogue." (As long as everybody does what The Man says.) And finally,

Five: "Political and cultural rights and social justice for all."

All noble aspirations and clearly an Indonesian work in progress. Kinda like America's Bill of Rights and Constitution.

After checking into our rooms at the altogether seedy looking *Hotel Indonesia*, I treated Andy to dinner. It was a lavish labor-intensive fifteen-course feast of traditional Indonesian *rijstaefel* at the only five-star restaurant in Jakarta. Pleasantly enough, the restaurant was called the *Oasis*. It sure was! The restaurant scored high points for its native visuals in the Dutch colonial setting and traditional national costume wear. But somewhere, somehow, something went seriously awry in the entertainment portion of the evening. Staggeringly overpriced drinks and the attack of the Wandering Minstrels, caused me to quake in my seat. Their Peruvian-accented version of "*O Sol e Mio*" was enough to cause a serious breach of peace in more civilized parts of the world. The noise they emitted smothered our usual blithe, carefree repartee. I was stunned, but the food was great!

It was during dinner that Andy and I discussed at length numerous plausible economic development strategies that might be employed by this Third World, verging on Fourth World status nation. Finally our IR graduate courses were paying off. Objective concepts and subjective ideas alike were all tossed into the wind and rolled off our tongues. We were using Freudian psychoanalysis and free association techniques with terms like: a basket-case, debt-for-nature swaps, neutron bombs, junk bonds, top-down elite rule, Chinese *Diaspora*, bottom-up economic planning, resource management, brain drain, population control, export-oriented economy, revolution of rising expectations, and just plain revolution, along with a more extreme, stopgap and ending with a desperate solution I unabashedly theorized as *selective metropolitan genocide.*

We were both at once overwhelmed by the possible social and political consequences of some of our thoughts actually being put into action. Thank goodness neither of us are officially commissioned diplomats. At least not yet anyway! But then again, if we won this madcap travel adventure scavenger hunt and contributed the winning bank roll to a worthy political campaign we might just be appointed an Ambassadorial commission. "*Mr. Ambassador, the Prime Minister will see you now…*" has a nice ring to it!? But alas, like all nobly undertaken political discussions, where honorable men inevitably tend to honorably disagree, this debate too was left without arriving at a mutually agreed upon consensus.

It was *o-dark-thirty* as we attempted a running start in our race in order to catch the first *Garuda* Airlines shuttle out of Jakarta. A single evening in this haunting metropolis was plainly far too much for our weary socially conscious souls. We had succumbed to a nasty dose of those insidious *Third World Blues.* We had to move on, and quickly we both thought. After a meaningless squabble between the gaudy Hotel Indonesia's head cashier and myself about a questionably excessive mini-bar bill, we caught a shuttle bus to the opulent and sprawling *Soekarno-Hatta* International Airport.

A super-kitsch monument to the abhorrent waste, fraud and abuse of foreign aid receipts. This ultra-modern grand facade was built to deceive the coming-and-going international dignitaries and business travelers alike, as to the capital city's 20th Century progress. The fact was that *it* was the only thing 20th Century-like in the entire metropolitan area. A classic case of an overindulgent Third World have-they-no-shame, kickback and graft *World Bank* construction project. Rumor has it from the man on the street, that the *Fluor* and *Bechtel* corporations both submitted the highest bids, and ultimately won the contract. And so it goes…the rich get richer and the poor get poorer.

Being half asleep as we drove through the still shadowy streets, we weren't really paying particularly close attention to "*AM Jakarta*" as it played on the airport bus's black and white in-dash mini-TV. It seemed pretty much like the usual insipid *blah-blah-blah* fare served up on any of those numerous AM-wake-you-up type of shows spreading like a bad disease throughout the entire known world: local weather reports; celebrity guests shamelessly plugging their latest book, movie or newest addition; routine regional news headlines; contemporary fashion pro-files (What the well dressed Muslim is wearing to the mosque. I kid you not!); and, a rather concisely worded volcano eruption warning for Mount Merpi, located in central Java.

That last tidbit of formidable geological news slashed across my groggy and inattentive head. I awoke Andy with an elbow to his lower ribcage.

Guess where we were heading? Yup, you guessed it, central Java! The ancient city of Yogyakarta to be exact. About twenty short kilometers away from a teed-off fiery mountain that was getting ready to rock 'n' roll. We were about to enter the infamous Indonesian *Ring of Fire*. Not wanting to read more into the potentially volatile situation than there actually was, I asked the bus driver to please explain this alert. I clearly required additional information to synthesize, so I could conduct an unbiased environmental impact statement, if you will.

Our able driver proceeded in more or less poetic verse, "When the ants come up from the ground and the tigers come down from the mountains…look out!" he animatedly cautioned us. We briefly paused to stare at each other with raised eyebrows, again sensing the apparent gravity of the situation. I marveled at this natural method of accurately forecasting seismic activity beneath the earth. Coming from earthquake conscious Southern California, I could well appreci-ate it. I wondered aloud if the US Geological Survey Team knew of this ancient scientific method!?

Then out of the blue and with a high-pitched voice Andy meekly queried him, "Tigers you say?"

"Yes sirs!" the driver flatly proclaimed with a toothy David Letterman-like grin.

"Great!" Andy said with reluctant resignation. I shrugged my shoulders with the weight of the situation.

As long time travel junkies who have wandered all the globe's continents. Okay, I'm exaggerating just a bit here, neither of us have actually been to Antarctica. Although I have seen a few pictures of it from friends who went and that's, quite frankly, as close as I ever want to get to the frigid barren land. We had however, to the best of our recollection, never come across such a formidable warning as this particular one. Sure enough, in our past geopolitical escapades we've had to deal with numerous natural and man-made unpleasantries, such as: typhoon warnings and cyclone alerts, reports of river blindness and cholera outbreaks, drunken elephant stampedes, numerous bouts of ethnic strife, bandit alerts, polar-bear sightings, State Department travel warnings, military coups and counter-coups, shark attack warnings, the menacing odd terrorist threat, assorted forms of government repression, unhealthful urban sulfur dioxide emission alerts, acid rain, wild mountain fires, black ice and white outs, blinding desert sandstorms, flash flooding, food poisoning outbreaks, Alaskan mosquito attacks, bear warnings, unpredictable *El Nino* weather patterns, mud slides and even swarms of menacing locusts. But never a volcano eruption warning!

I later learned that Mount Merapi, which literally means Fire Mountain, was just one of over a hundred and twenty active volcanoes on the island of Java, that over the years, had claimed an estimated hundred and fifty thousand lives during their fiery molten lava eruptions. In fact, of the 850 active volcanoes worldwide, a full twenty percent are located in Indonesian.

This overly sensationalized television warning may have been a useful public service announcement designed for the local's consumption, but we wandering global voyeurs on a divine mission from JB shrugged it off in no uncertain terms. In one ear and out the other. Tempting fate by rebelliously thumbing our nose at the potentially perilous situation. Provoking divine providence by asking the all apparent question: What could we possibly do about it anyway? Absolutely nothing, we ultimately concluded. Except for not going to the spiritual capital city of ancient Java, and that was completely out of the question. It was a non-issue. We were not to be deterred in our dedicated quest for a high placing finish in the Human*Race*. Life or limb be damned!

The race was entering an entirely different, altogether more formidable phase, that of mother nature versus the *scavenger hunt from hell*. We were on the clubhouse stretch.

Ever notice that the more out-of-the-way you wander from the centers of the civilized world the smaller the airplanes seem to get? I do! On this particularly battered technological dinosaur of a DC-9 there were no pre-assigned seats. And that's where the similarity with the *Trump Shuttle* ends. Advance reservations are but a pipe dream, a fiction in this part of the world. It was strictly a first come, first sit affair. When all the seats are occupied, and that can take several hours, then, and only then, does the plane leave. Just that simple. They could teach those rude gate agents at hustling and bustling JFK International a thing or two about handling customer complaints. Andy said he had dreamt of flying on the *SST Concorde* the night before, pronouncing that "It's so much more civilized traveling twice as fast as a popping champagne cork." I quickly slapped him in the face with reality. "Propellers dude. Remember them?" I don't want to say that I was nervous about our impending flight, but…I did check to make sure that the little pink DMV organ donor card had been correctly filled out, signed and witnessed. Eyes, kidneys, heart and liver all checked. Shit, who would want my shriveled up liver I thought? Not that there'd be anything left to donate anyway. The tigers would make sure of that.

We also noticed, much to our collective dismay, that our carry-on rucksacks had once again expanded overnight. Not a good sign when you're participating in a long distance endurance race. Over the past several days the tacky tourist trophies we had been accumulating as part of the scavenger hunt requirements were beginning to multiply with increased vigor and were starting to weigh us down. I was also reluctantly forced to agree with Andy that, in retrospect, that *Playboy* for a six-pack of beer exchange that I had made the previous night with the *Hotel Indonesia's* horny and all-too-willing concierge, was probably not in our best strategic interests. "But hey, they were imported *Molson Canadian* lagers!" I rationalized, with Andy nodding in reluctant agreement. We ever so carefully stowed our temporarily bulky luggage under the seat in front of us. *Swiss Army* knife bottle opener near by and ready.

Soon velvety-green layered rice paddies with beasts of burden plowing fields, narrow dirt roads busy with horse carriages, bicycles and trishaws, lushly dense tropical jungles dotted with rusted brown corrugated metal houses, deep river gorges, water buffalo, goats and children, lots of children, could be seen from our aerial vantage point as we hopped along the smoldering tops of the volcano-dotted terrain. We were headed for places so utterly remote from our daily urban American realities for a rather abrupt lesson in 10th Century Southeast Asian history *terra incognito* extraordinarie. This was a civilization of timeless ancient ways with traditional community values centered around a self-sufficient agrarian-based economy. And, last but not least, a land of dedicated and extremely faithful believers.

The Indonesian archipelago, a sprawling diverse collection of over thirteen thousand islands scattered across the far eastern reaches of the Indian Ocean to Northern Australia, is an interesting religious paradox. Although it is a self-proclaimed Islamic nation, you do in fact notice and encounter mostly Hindu's, Buddhists and Christians, the latter of which is a self-professed seriously non-Islamic proselytizing religion.

The nation's self-anointed motto of *Bhinneka Tunggal Ika,* is loosely translated into Unity in Diversity. An apt description for the kaleido-scope of peoples that we witnessed first hand.

Yogyakarta must surely be one of the world's largest villages weighing in with over three million residents in the surrounding environs. It still remains small however, by all our Western urban standards. No tall buildings hovering over the palm trees. No fast food establishments serving each corner, save for a chain of always moving Fast Freddies' *satay* stands. No multi-cineplex's or frozen yogurt outlets. And for the most part, the locals' preferred mode of transportation is via foot, bicycle, *becaks* or water buffalo cart. Yogya as the locals call it, is also the spiritual and cultural capital of the island of Java. It is located in the center of what is known as the *Realm of the Dead,* which is home to several fasci-nating ancient holy ruins and sacred cemeteries. But art seems to be the main draw in Yogya. Dancers, musicians, poets, painters, *batik* silk scarf makers, puppeteers and craftsman, have all been drawn to this focal point of Indonesian culture.

We unsuccessfully tried to negotiate a better price for the services of a local taxicab driver for a couple of hours. The lackluster commercial competition that took place at the *Yogyakarta-Adisucipto* National Airport, was between several entrepreneurs whose price quotes were all the same. For a few minutes I felt like Monty Hall doing his *"Let's Make A Deal"* game-show shtick with no one taking Door Number One…Price-fixing, I then ventured was only an American ideal and solely an FTC *Anti-Trust Act* violation. I must in all honesty say, that we did try to charter a helicopter conveniently located at the Yogya airport. It was a little pricey though. We eventually acquiesced to their high pressure tactics and got a rather run-down brown cab. Quickly, we set out to do this fairytale-like land. Two cyberpunks from the land of *Milk and Honey* and the *Home of the Brave* had come a calling.

In quick succession we visited a talented Kasongan Village potter named Marco Polo and stopped off at temple after ancient temple in the surrounding area. We cruised past ox-carts, elderly Javanese women balancing huge packs on their heads, and children. Lot's of children! We noticed a lot of older women humped over bearing woven bamboo baskets on their backs. We finally headed towards the lively sprawling downtown market they called *Pasar Beringharjo*, located on Malioboro Street across from the Night Market and down the street from the Sultan's Palace. While strolling through the market, I noticed an unusual array of lounging dharma bums, frenzied antique collectors, conspiring German exporters, Santa Fe Zen masters and dozens of has-been wannabes taking in the local carnival-like atmosphere.

It was here, amidst the exotic aromas and sweet scents of a Third World market, that we arranged for passage via overland mini-bus to the mystical, tropical Island of Bali. We would unfortunately miss out on several other key cultural, historic and spiritual finds in this part of Central Java. We had even heard that *Hamengkubuwono X*, the Sultan of the Yogya area, had desired to meet some Human*Racers* during our quick pass through the region. It would have to be somebody else though because we had a bus to catch.

It's funny how we sometimes feel about exotic places such as Yogya. Sometimes you feel as though you are cast into a mesmerizing spell. Be it one of infatuation, or just cultural disorientation, I don't really know. But it creates a certain dilemma for the would-be traveler. Like a new lover, there are times when you really don't want to get to know them any better. For the more scrutiny you give them, the more you destroy the mystery of it all. You know that old saying, *familiarity breeds contempt*…Yogya gave me that feeling. But in this particular case, I would have liked to get to know it a lot better. Could it be true love? Or just a mild infatuation? I would one day return I thought.

And so, with the suddenness of an Indonesian rainstorm we left Yogya. Booked on an odyssey of sight and sound that many racers later felt was either the highlight or nadir, depending entirely upon one's own mental constitution and intestinal fortitude, of their entire round-the-world adventure: the now notorious eighteen-hour ride through mountainous central Java en route to the city of Denpasar on the island of Bali.

While traveling on this so-called "Executive Class" bus, we rode over four hundred gruesome miles into the place where life may have begun. If you can remember way back to your high school anthropology lessons, *Homo erectus* aka *Java Man*, made this, the Solo River region, his home. But it's also a place that somewhere along the way, time had forgotten. It was during this fantastic voyage through the very heart of Java that we became excessively pensive, philosophically dazed and emotionally reflective as to our personal intentions and expressed purpose.

This first leg, (The Human*Race* was divided into four separate legs: Southeast Asia, the Middle East, Europe and the USA.) for us proved to be by far the most interesting and entertaining. Due, in retrospect, to the undeniable fact that we weren't totally jaded as of yet! It was still fresh, exotic and somewhat fun.

Thus far, on this first leg, we had deftly sought out such treasures as: a questionable organic aphrodisiac from an occult herbal medicine shop on Hong Kong's Kowloon peninsula. If the truth be told, Andy just couldn't bring himself around to effectively negotiate for the sliced-off tip of a fellow mammal's penis. Walrus I think it was! We had cornered a mysterious soothsayer that went by the name of Tamul Moothy in a seedy-looking back alley in the Little India section of Singapore. His ever clever sales pitch hook was having a brilliant green parrot choose our personalized fortunes with his chipped beak. "Oooh, how very scientific and New Age," chorused my past-life-regression-voice-as-a-Greek philosopher. Or was it as a Mongolian stable boy? We also had our palms read and our tea leaves analyzed, and had a laid off financial analyst-*cum*-numerologist compute our futures. The only thing we didn't do was attend a spooky seance session in a rundown specialty spiritual shop in Singapore. Both of us were given contradictory mixed reviews in the psychic skills department. Our foretold futures ran the gambit from fame and fortune, to a life of crime and an early grave. Like most professions, I guess, confusion reigns.

Before, or maybe it was later, we located the spiritual burial grounds of Islamic sultans in Indonesia, and had tracked down the last cobbler on earth who crafts petite miniature footwear for aristocratic Chinese women who've had their feet mercilessly bound since birth. We found the latter, a pygmy-sized *S & M* enthusiast named Yeo Sing Guat in comfortable exile from China, his home since the 1949 Maoist revolution, in a remote little fishing village on the pirate west coast of Malaysia. Incredibly, Mr. Yeo boasts, with his sinister toothless smile, that he still services around a dozen or so clients!

It was also in Southeast Asia that we were charged with the unsavory task of draping deadly venomous Wagler's pit vipers on our bodies. It was to be a good luck gesture offering to the gods at the now famous tourist attraction, aptly named Snake Temple, officially known as the *Temple of the Azure Cloud* on the Island of Pulau Pinang, located just south of the Thai-Malay border. The snakes were allegedly bombed on temple incense. Two grams of Valium seemed more like it! Notwithstanding the relative safety of the situation, we flipped a coin for this privileged photo op. I lost! Thanks to a childhood friend named Pat McDonald from my hometown of Windsor, Ontario, I am scared to death of snakes. Andy laughed a hardy laugh at my expense. It was over none too soon for my taste. Andy then took his sweet old time and for some reason couldn't correctly focus the camera. "Paybacks a bitch," I warned him and I always get even too. For those keeping track so far, the updated *Whirled Tour '89* scoreboard reads: Valvur 2-Chalmers 0.

Another of this leg's man-at-one-with-nature highlights took place during a group photo session with a rather elderly and balding, red-headed orangutan. Being quick on our feet and resourcefully cunning single-men of the eighties, not to mention short a blowdart gun and much too busy to go off trekking through the dense snake-infested tropical rainforests, we tracked down a particularly tame primate named *Ah Meng* at the Singapore Zoo. (See cover. That's Andy in the middle!) Like those hastily staged scenes out of a Marlin Perkins' *"Mutual of Omaha Wild Kingdom"* episode, all three of us smiled and held hands. I stuffed a few bills in her keeper's shirt pocket...and we were off to the next scavenge.

During the exhausting Southeast Asia segment, we were also charged with finding amusing, and at times, utterly perplexing scavenges. Among them, we ferreted out such odd ball objects as: a *hakka* hat worn by the widowed women of a certain Chinese sect; a deformed S-shaped fish called *Dragon Horse Toman*; brass ear cleaning spoons that when heated melt the wax out of your ear; hell money for funeral offerings and dragon joss sticks. Ambrose Bierce's *"Devil's Dictionary"* defines joss sticks as "small sticks burned by the Chinese in their pagan tom foolery, in imitation of certain sacred rites of our holy religion." We discovered many delightful and tropical fruits, with strange names like: *nanka, salak, durian* (Smells like hell and tastes like heaven!) and *mangosteen*. And came across numerous types of specially designed and indigenously made pottery. We visited way too many temples, pagodas, shrines and mosques for our secular humanist enjoyment. And finally, indulged in a few, way too few for our hungry tastes buds, exotic dinners, such as the ones we devoured at the *Banana Leaf* in Singapore or the men-only *Bird Restaurant* establishment in Hong Kong.

We also had the unforgettable pleasure of visiting the ancient town of Yogyakarta, located in the center of the Island of Java. This remote Indonesian village turned out to be a place that wasn't adequately described in all it's grandeur in our usually trusty *Michelin* guidebook. As I stated earlier, it's a place with a strange spiritual and aesthetic allure. From Paragtritis Beach in the south to the *batik* shop lined streets surrounding Surgo Road, Yogya is an exhilarating environment to be in. It was one of the few spots that Andy and I had visited during this journey that we both agreed that we'd like to return to some other time for an extended stay. A unique fairytale-like place where you can experience the historic architectural and spiritual ruins of the *Temple of Borobudur.*

Borobudur, built around 778 CE, (*Current Era* is used in this text as opposed to 778 AD, which is a tad ethnocentric on our parts. Especially when talking sacred sites of other religions.) is an awe-inspiring five-story colossal and cosmic monument to the gods carved from black molten lava. Mysterious and stunning, it is reputed to be the "largest Buddhist sanctuary in the world." It is also considered one of the celebrated Seven Wonders of the Middle World. (*Quick, name the other six!?*) The graffiti-inspired sign outside the complex read:

"Closed from 800 AD to 1983 AD Now opened [sic] *from 6:00 a.m. to 6:00 p.m."* In an apparent reference to the fact that this spiritual masterpiece was once abandoned and covered by volcanic soot for about a thousand years.

Luckily it was raining and we were able to witness a spectacular display of the hundreds of spooky gargoyle-like spouts that surround the ancient temple, spewing blasts of water at potential demons within our midst. On each level of the pyramid a fascinating collection of stone carved bell-shaped enclosures surround and cover hundreds of hidden Buddhas. From the top of Borobudur you can see vast green fields and the mighty volcanoes nearby guarding this temple. As I gazed at the hundreds of stone relief's depicting Buddha, this white foreign devil was left in awe at the grandeur of Borobudur Temple. It was a definite spiritual powerspot. It was also funny watching Andy get spat at by the gargoyles, coincidence? I think not!

Built sometime around the 8th Century, unfortunately there's no dated corner-stone anywhere on the site, the three hundred and forty-five step high *Mount Imogiri* located south of Yogya, is the sacred royal burial grounds of the ancient Javanese Sultans. Like a ladder leading us up into the heavens above, we climbed the steep steps of this ancient *Forest Lawn.* Awaiting us at the top with cool cups of well water, were sarong-draped holy priest-guards. We sat for a moment and chatted

with these guardians while we caught our breaths. They blessed us and
we descended from this eerie place, as quickly as we had arrived, but
much more attuned to the spiritual makeup of this magnificently
ancient region.

Wonders of the Middle World
Pantheon, Italy
Taj Mahal, India
Angkor Wat, Cambodia
Borobodur Temple, Java
Chartres, France
Great Wall, China
Machu Picchu, Peru

Also uncovered surrounding Yogya, were the two bewitching *Boko*
and *Prambanan Temples*. The latter being a ninth century complex
made up of over two hundred and forty Hindu-Javanese shrines. These
profoundly mysterious places exhibit, for those adventurous enough to
come meandering off the beaten path, enduring picturesque impressions
of indisputable architectural brilliance; an unparalleled ancient culture
and an extremely fascinating, yet wholly enigmatic concoction of religious myths. All of which are clearly beyond the grasp of the six-second
sound-bite mentality of our Western *Empty-V* generation from which
we come.

It was while visiting breathtaking Borobudur and then later as we
hastily galloped across the heavenly lush Island of Bali, that our frazzled
consciences became increasingly torn as to just what exactly we were
doing to the world.

The Past Being Prologue

A little background is due here. In many ways the 1989 Human*Race* was the culmination of what Andy and I had been unwittingly preparing ourselves for over the last several years. Clearly, we now both realized that this adventure on wasn't one of those run of the mill two-week dial *1(800)FUN-TIME*, single destination all-inclusive beach holidays. Despite the trip's inherent fun, it took preparing for and tons of planning. Luckily, our life was all the planning and preparing we needed for the Human*Race*.

Andy and I met at graduate school in the San Francisco Bay area. And no, we're not gay. Not that there's anything wrong with that! But it was while we were studying the more arcane aspects of international relations, (We jokingly referred to it as alligator farming for some unknown reason!?) that we discovered our mutual wanderlust for places off the beaten track.

Shortly thereafter we embarked on our original *Whirled Tour*. It took us from San Francisco to Tokyo, Taiwan, Bangkok and Pattaya, Thailand, or should I say as others do *Thigh*land?, and back in six short days! Try explaining that to a suspicious US Customs officer who notices that you perfectly match the US Government's so-called drug-courier profile. "Honest sir, we just wanted to windsurf the Gulf of Siam for a few days." After that, it seemed only natural for us to attend the initial pre-*glasnost* Reagan-Gorbachev Summit in the Fall of 1985 in Geneva, Switzerland. There we sat by the piano bar at the *Beau Rivage* Hotel enjoying the black n' white ivory stylings of USIA Director

Charles Wick, along with a few other lounge lizards by the name of *ABC News* President Roone Arlidge, and his bushy eye-browed Paris correspondent, Pierre Salinger. The entertainment cover charge nearly killed us though. Being the *Summit Junkies* we were, we also hung out with *ABC's* Sam and Ted, and the whole *Gang of Network Three*: Rather, Jennings and Brokow. Oh I'm quite sure that they'll all deny any knowledge or recollection of us or this. But, we have the negatives to prove it! This adventure was deemed an extra-credit field trip while I was continuing my postgraduate studies in political economics at the legendary hot-bed of international democratic-socialism, the *London School of Economics* (LSE), in England.

Since then, we've become stopover artists, and together we've done the much celebrated pre-Lenten *Carnaval* extravaganza in Rio, without advance reservations I'd like to add! Sipped the grapes from the vineyards of the *Bourgogne* region of France on our *"We'll Sign For It Tour,"* and danced on table-tops in difficult to find after hours Istanbul discotheques in Asia Minor on my 30th birthday. Between the two of us, we've chased humpback whales down to Scammons Lagoon in Baja and partied till daybreak at Montego Bay's annual pot-induced reggae *Sunsplash Music Festival*. Island hopped the Greek Isles on windsurfers with only olives, dates, crusty bread and *ouzo* for substance. Roamed the snow capped High Atlas mountains surrounding the desert oasis of Marrakech. Hiked along the Inca Trail to Machu Picchu. Crossed glaciers, volcanic craters and geyser fields in other worldly Iceland. Rode elephants through the thick jungles adjacent to the Golden Triangle. Boated along such great rivers as the remote Rajang River of Borneo, the Mekong through central Laos, the Orinoco of Venezuela and the mighty Irrawaddy River of Burma. Along with these travel adventures, we've visited such other marvelous world-class international destinations as: Sydney, Dublin, Karachi, Seoul, Teheran, Budapest, Tangiers, Chiang Mai, New Guinea, Yangon, Tokyo, Athens and Caracas, to name but a few.

Domestically, we've covered equally interesting ground, visiting the likes of: hallowed Tiger Stadium, kooky Key West, sunny Cabo, mosquito plagued Lake Athabasca (Where I witnessed the celestial pyrotechnics of the sublimely colorful *aurora borealis.*), the 1984 Democratic National Convention (Where we oversaw the nomination process of the Demo's sacrificial lamb, Walter Mondale!), visited blistering hot Pahrump, Nevada (Where we ran contraband across the state line near Death Valley.), and we've actually seen race cars race at the Indy 500, visited both the pre and post-eruption Mt. St. Helen's area, bare-backed across the Great Divide, visited Moose Jaw, Maui, toured *Graceland* and the Blues Delta, hung out at Quebec's Winter Carnival, kayaked the San Juan Islands, trolled the neon lit streets of Las Vegas and of course, camped outside the retro-chic Santa Fe area. And somewhere along the way, we were involuntary participants in a pre-*Harmonic Convergence* power spot seminar for lonely suburban housewives.

Our underlying travel perspective is: it isn't how much time you actually spend somewhere that makes it an unforgettable experience, but it's how you spend your time there that matters. Life, is but the sum of moments. And we have had some very special moments while traveling. We're not just consumers of time and takers of space in this life. *Carpe diem,* as the ancient Greeks said, is our on-the-road motto. Now Andy claims to have never actually heard me ever say *carpe diem,* and thinks that my real travel motto is "...*two more beers please!*" He has a legitimate point too.

Needless to say then, together we've become seasoned and highly resourceful, yet hopelessly addicted travel junkies. Suffering from wanderlust squared. Global grazers if you will. "Have passport and *American Express* card will travel," read our lengthy respective travel adventure resumes. At any rate, we are internationally educated, culturally literate, semi-in-shape, fashion conscious, economically enterprising and well-mannered members of the luckiest of generations, the post-war Baby Boomers. Fully enjoying all the fruits of our parents hard labors, and I might add, the longest peacetime economic expansion in American history, during these final days in the Age of Reagan Excess at the height of the American Empire. Not that we're bragging or anything.

We have learned, through lengthy bouts of trial and error, to complement each other extremely well on the road, as we played off of each others strengths—and continually point out each others weaknesses—in a collective attempt to achieve a more fulfilling travel experience. Whenever and wherever we venture to. This special combination of our collective past experiences makes us both undeniably self-sufficient and wholly independent. Yet, over the years, while we've traveled the globe and seen it's seven seas and climbed many of it's humanistic peaks, we have consciously created a division of labor in order to maximize our potential.

Andy is the: food taster, travel agent, nagging conscience, road entertainment, editor, best friend and linguist extraordinaire. And Andy would tell you, one would hope, that I am the official: body guard, music and video electronic engineer, strategic planner, chief scrounger, money manager, cartographer, best friend and international financial advisor. He's the Sixties era New-Bohemian *I'm okay, you're okay…*gestalt psychologist type and I'm more the Eighties rationalists, existential and pragmatic enjoy-life-while-you-can philosopher. We're both voracious readers who will consume just about anything that is put in front of us from the hard news *Wall Street Journal* to our buddy Paul Krassner's irreverent rag *The Realist*. Either one of us will walk for hours in order to get our hands on a recent edition of the *New York Times* or a copy of *The Nation*. I've got enough *chutzpah* for both of us plus two or three, and he has enough urbane charm, not to mention deep gray-blue eyes, to get us out of the situations that I get us into. A typical conversation between Andy and I on the road goes something like this:

Andy: "Gee Bill, the sign we just passed says KEEP OUT."

Bill: "So? I'm just taking a picture."

Andy: "But Bill, here comes some guy. Does he look happy to you? He's got a shiny blue gun too!"

You get the picture…

He travels light and borrows from me everything that he should have brought for himself. I'm a dutiful former Boy Scout, so I'm always prepared. And Andy's a former flight attendant, so he makes great cheese and crackers and can always open a bottle of *vino*. Simply put, the synergy that we create together produces a real dynamic duo on the road. And this creates some real life on-the-road adventures. *Batman and Robin* have nothing on us.

As you can no doubt ascertain then, it seemed that we had trained the better part of our adult lives for this chance to formally display our travel savvy and enter this first of its kind Human*Race*. I remember first learning of JB's great race idea in the late Spring of 1989. I was on a plane, en route to London and a hot *rendavouz* weekend with a rather leggy Icelandic blonde, reading the Travel section of the bulky Sunday *New York Times*. Excited, I immediately called Andy upon my arrival at *Heathrow's Terminal Three* and relayed the novel idea to him. He too, was immediately turned on by the very notion of a scavenger hunt race around the world. We both agreed to enter the race and to figure out the financial details later. As usual, when there's a will, there's a way!

That done, and now actually partaking in this wacky race, what we hadn't anticipated however, was how we'd feel along our way to possible fame and fortune. A metamorphosis took place that transformed us, from him being a high-browed political humorist (read: stand-up comic) and provocative socialite-novelist-playwright, and me, from a practicing radical political economist (read: unelected, unappointed and un-employed policy maker posing as a businessman) and vice-ridden ex-jock, into a couple of, dare I say it, oh my God no not us, *cultural terrorists*! We had somehow evolved into a cross between an international version of "*Bonnie and Clyde*" and "*Easy Rider*."

It seemed to be an insidious conversion at first. Subtle and entirely subconscious in nature, but one that took place nonetheless, seemingly without a lot of conscientious objecting to on our part also. Was it the result of the obvious scent of truly ruthless competition in the air? Was it the mercenary allure of the twenty-thousand dollars (*Originally $25,000 and reduced by JB the day before the event!*) in prize money? Or, was it simply our heavily ingrained cultural arrogance showing it's true colors? Neither of us had any ready made answers for the uncomfortable thought provoking state we were now in. But we unquestionably understood what was happening to us. And we didn't enjoy it one bit.

Picture this if you will: There we were, in some out-of-the-way exotic and peaceful location in Indonesia, visiting yet another Hollywood type-cast emerging Third World benign dictatorship. An economically impoverished, yet culturally and spiritually rich environment. A place where people smiled with straightforward sincerity as you passed. A place where their apparently instinctive and inquisitive minds put forth simple, yet thought provoking and puzzling questions. Questions concerning some of our numerous cultural differences arose; such as: "Why do you travel so far away from your home land? Don't you like your home?" Or "You should have many babies. Where are your wives?" and "Why did you grow hair on your face? Do you have an ugly head?" Out of the mouths of babes. In a few words, it is a place where prized personal material possessions, as scant and paltry as they were, are happily and readily shared among friends, family and strangers alike. A place where personal conversations between two strangers, though labored by the obvious language difficulties, were nonetheless undertaken and became an enriching educational event in their and our lives. A place where they smile when they're in pain. It was, simply put, a place where mutual respect and courteous behavior were the expected norm of social interaction, not the exception.

And there we were, wearing our obscurely glib neon-colored political T-shirts in support of the *Afghani freedom fighters* or *Earth Day 1990.* Wearing chicly tattered *Levi* 501 jeans; *Nike* Air Jordan cross training running shoes and sporting *Los Angeles Lakers* championship baseball caps. All the while laboring under the usual leisure-time paraphernalia of about a half-a-ton of rather expensive and highly sophisticated audio and video equipment strapped to our shoulders and sprinting across their exceptionally sacred burial grounds, ancient historical monuments, archeological wonders and treasured cultural museums alike, while barking out perplexing questions and dictatorial commands. All in a vicious attempt to obtain yet another meaningless tourist trophy and avail ourselves of yet another pretentious photo-op! *"Been there. Done that. What's next?"* was our newly acquired racing motto. Or more to the point: *"We came. We saw. We consumed. We're outta here!"*

We'd become unwitting traveling emissaries of our land, Ambassadors if you will, exposing the true spirit of our throw-away mentality and scurrilous societal upbringing. With attention spans limited to a three-and-a-half minute music video. *Attention Deficit Disorder* (ADD), I think they call it!? The ugly American at play once again. Strangers in an even stranger land. But, being full blown cultural terrorists wasn't just exclusively American tourists' private domain anymore. That is, to insult the entire population of the known world and corrupt the locals by throwing the color of money around. *Pax Americana* is no more. The highly sophisticated $250 billion-a-year global tourism industry has a new international marketing gimmick called adventure tourism. And its catchy hook has helped spread the blame around. It was now the collective irresponsibility of all the globe-trotting, adventurous and *nouveau riche* Germans, French and the Yuppie Japanese generation as well. *Homo touristicus* all. And at its very worst.

We liked to think of ourselves at least, as Noble Savages. Graduates of the *Alan Alda School For The Sensitive Traveler.* Why, we had even studied geography, and could actually point to a map and tell you where remote places like Lago Titicaca, Mombassa or Uluru are. We also had studied world religions at our fine liberal arts colleges. We were keenly aware of the political sensitivities, as well as the extremely fragile domestic tranquillity, of our host foreign environments. We sincerely tried along the way to be thoughtful, courteous and conscientious. We tried not to be hopelessly chauvinistic in our frivolous endeavor. No matter how gonzo we acted with ourselves and other contestants at times, we approached the indigenous population with a certain degree of humility on our parts.

We understood that the basic human emotions of disgust, anger, fear, sadness and happiness, are all universal feelings to varying degrees. I knew what caused me to be disgusted or angered in other peoples behavior and I wasn't going to replicate those unsightly behaviors while traveling. We listened to what the locals had to say. Tried to be honorable gentlemen and not make any insincere or false promises. In fact, we clearly understood that we were totally vulnerable to their sense of goodwill. Wrong directions, inaccurate information or worse, could have been our plight and becoming losers our destiny. We had a well cultivated sense of travel ethics, if you will. Together, we both traveled under the utopian dictum of: "He who runs cannot walk with dignity..." to paraphrase a vintage "*Kung Fu*" episode. Yet the reckless haste at which we were now traveling created a definite dilemma for us.

Do we just completely abandon any sense of traveling decorum we may have had? Or, do we struggle to maintain an expressed sentiment of common mutual respect and reverence for the places we visited? These modest questions created quite an intellectual and moral quandary for us. They led us to take a personality inventory of sorts.

We both acknowledge the so-called *exchange theory* of interpersonal relationships. We know that in each and every encounter we have with the local folk, that in some way we both obtain something from them, as well as leave something behind in our wakes. Our goal then, was to not willfully and knowingly commit any cultural *faux pas*, as the French so elegantly call them. No, Andy and I weren't going to bribe (Well, not any more than we would back in the Good Olde USA anyway!), rape or pillage, like so many of our chauvinistic Eurocentric Colonial-minded predecessors that had come before us. We weren't about to leave behind any ill-will or spiritual pollution, highly contagious information anxieties, techophobias, *Chronic Fatigue Syndromes*, or existential Nowism philosophies.

We wouldn't disrupt the local economy by recklessly throwing money around and over paying; foster any regional tribal resentment by hitting on their women, nor inflate local societal expectations. We wouldn't litter the countryside with our discarded *Evian* water bottles, or act in any sort of head-scratching, outlandishly abhorrent way, as our part of the special transaction, in exchange for savory tastes of their remarkably rich culture, a profound recognition of their unique historical perspective, enjoying their beautiful and exotic landscapes, and the simple enjoyment of connecting on a very basic human and personal level. Clearly, our well ingrained white liberal Judeo-Christian guilt ethic just simply wouldn't allow it to happen. We would not succumb to the highly suspect *ends justifies the means* ethos.

Looking back, I don't really know if we succeeded in this worthy endeavor while engaging in heated competition during the entire race. We may have had isolated lapses of conscience. But I do know that we genuinely tried. We did travel and compete in a true spirit of humility and heeded carefully our global hosts.

Others competing in the Human*Race* weren't as noble we soon learned. We would inevitably meet up with some of our racing competitors, either at specific scavenges or at the inevitable transportation bottlenecks. These turned out to be perversely savage happenings. Some of our fellow participants acted the role of the not-so-innocents-abroad. Wholly unsubstantiated rumors and equally nasty innuendo proliferated. This produced a whole new meaning to the rigors of the battle term *RUMINT*, rumor intelligence. These seemingly friendly and well-mannered professional people, when schmoozing with the local media at a cocktail party in San Francisco, turned into, what Hunter S. Thompson would aptly paraphrase I think as: rabid jackals running amok in the jungles of the Third World urban legends. Whatever that means? Pity the poor techno-illiterate natives who crossed their paths.

We would both openly and secretly observe, while I was wearing my Army surplus *Bee-A-Tree* camouflage kit, contestants throughout the course of the hunt throwing their bloated sense of cultural superiority around. It was like watching animal-like Mike Tyson mercilessly pounding on a powerless Woody Allen-like figure in the ring for twelve rounds. And the ref wouldn't stop the fight! It was without a doubt, a hideous scene to glimpse. Karmic debris flew in every direction.

I witnessed unrestrained team members berating and yelling at local merchants and customer service reps who weren't attuned to their highly sophisticated frantic race clocks. Clearly a much needed attitude check was in order. One ingrained image we viewed was of a mad dash across a tropical airport's tarmac followed by an unabashed flying of the green in an obnoxious attempt to procure whatever was necessary to capitalize on even just a paltry few minutes of advantage. (For some of the folks participating in the race, money was clearly no object!) It would have made the unscrupulous lads working in the pork-belly trading pits of the *Chicago Mercantile Exchange* cringe in a degenerate form of penis envy.

In one characteristic encounter we learned that Chalmers and Valvur were allegedly far ahead of the pack. "Bali!" we were told. "Or maybe even Egypt by now?" These uninformed racers were just regurgitating scuttlebutt that they had heard not fully comprehending the fact that we *were* Chalmers and Valvur and we *were* with them, in Singapore!

These rumors of racing intrigue, sabotage, team cheating and obnoxious behavior became part of the Human*Race*, just as sure as we were all members of the human race itself. We surmised, correctly or incorrectly at the time, that the prize money at the end of this global rainbow was the root cause. Nonetheless, some of the boorish behavior was clearly inexcusable and we believed that karma, in the end, demonstrated to be both an exceptionally humbling and especially equalizing force to be reckoned with. Not everyone was a loser (No pun intended!) in the race, some great fun folks had also entered.

Bali Ha'i, circa 1989

If Bali is indeed heaven on earth as some claim, then we were slogging through purgatory to get there. Right about now Andy and I were dining in purgatory's version of a diner. It wasn't awful, and the food was somewhat decent, if not instantly unrecognizable. I personally would have preferred a charred-broiled double-cheese *Fatburger* with grilled onions and greasy french fries thank you very much. But when you're in the middle of tiger, volcano and headhunter country, you give thanks for the little things. Like the fact that *we* weren't dinner!

But in all honesty, I don't think that it would be appropriate to actually call the open-air roadside eating establishment, along primitive Java's version of *Route 66*, a qualified American greasy spoon. Owing largely to the fact that Indonesian food is for the most part grease free. No, this hut-sized Indonesian-style truck stop, perched on the main east-west highway in volcano strewn central Java, was more like a muddy chop stick. It reminded me of the famous *Star Wars* intergalactic bar scene. I'm certain the mini-bus driver received a handsome kickback of a thousand or so *rupiahs* just for stopping his twelve passenger carriage here, and ate for free to boot, no doubt.

We had the distinct pleasure of eating food that not even our discriminating culinary taste buds could easily identify. "Oh the aroma! Oh the texture! Oh the spices!" Andy humorously intoned. "Give me a hint!" I shot back, "Was this animal, mineral or vegetable? Did it fly, crawl or swim here?" I fully employed Andy's food tasting expertise here. We tried to be gracious guests at this almost surreal dusty roadside eatery in the middle of the Javanese jungle in the shadow of a really large volcano, and eventually ate petite-sized portions of everything that was served to us on banana-leaf placemats. To the best of our collective knowledge however, we may have indulged in some sort of primordial soup. All the locals traveling with us laughed with our every bite of food. Did they know something we should have?

And all this whining from a man who regularly eats raw fish and barbecues elk! Where was my sense of adventure? Sure, we couldn't tell what it was, but it was hot and it was actually good! Later we heard from other racers who had stopped at similar places on their way to paradise that they had been served bowls of maggots. Really, *maggots*? Not everyone can prepare maggots. They have to be cooked just right. I have eaten at many questionable places around the world and have never gotten sick. I trust the local food within reason. The key is to trust the locals.

Restaurant Eating Tips
Never eat where you sleep…get out and mingle!
Never eat at a restaurant with a skinny chef!
When using your hands to eat, only use your right hand!
If you can't see water, don't order fish!
Stay away from food buffets…old food, irregular
temperatures and mass produced.
Make friends with the chef ASAP, he will make you
great special dishes!
Don't recognize what you're eating? Wait till after
you've finished to ask what it was!
If you can't boil it, peel it or grill it, don't eat it!
Be a fearless eater, try everything at least once!
10% of you *will* get sick abroad, one word-*Imodium*!

Traveling for twelve straight sleepless hours on a noisy bus that honked it's damn horn clear across Eastern Java into the wee small hours of the night, I wondered continually as to our exact whereabouts. It's times like these, I thought to myself, that I should have surgically implanted that small high frequency *406 megahertz* computerized GPS beacon chip into the frontal lobes of my brain. To think that with but a scratch of my head I could have instantly contacted those dutiful men and women of the *International Search and Rescue Team* via the geosynchronous orbiting *SARSAT* global satellite tracking system. The colorful sales brochure that I was sent about a year or so ago, boastfully claimed that they can verify your exact global longitude, latitude and elevation coordinates to within 40 meters. Sounds mighty impressive. A global electronic version of leaving bread crumbs behind. And they threw in an atomic alarm clock to boot! And to think it was a bargain at the time, and only would have cost me $1,995. I'm sure it was even cheaper at the Tokyo duty-free!

I finally got my bearings when we stopped to board an overbooked island-hopping ferry from Ketapang, on the Island of Java across the Bali Straits to Gillmanuk, a small coastal town on the Island of Bali. This small Java seaport was our gateway to the tropical and mysteriously enchanting home of two-and-a-half million islanders. We too would call it home, for at least a few days, we hoped. Our timing was exquisitely perfect. Sunrise! A remarkably special time in Third World agrarian-based societies. We were standing at the edge of Eden.

The unbroken eternal morning rhythm of Balinese life slowly exploded around us as we drove into Denpasar. All of a sudden you're surrounded by the beautifully radiant pre-morning light and able to witness an incredible array of eye-pleasing sights. Steamy equatorial mist hovered over the paddy-terraced ravines burning with the color of pinkish-red. Playful groups of children were wearing blue-gray uniforms jostling and jabbering on their way to school. The ever ominous volcanic mountains were silhouetted against the purple-pink sky, the tall sturdy palm trees and other exotic plants. Elderly women, teeth yellowed from chewing sugar cane, carried water buckets with great precision back to their humble abodes. Smoke, silvery-gray in color, bellowed from the green and brown thatched roof houses that lined the scenic low-lying valleys. Duck-herders were guiding their flocks with long bamboo poles towards lime green ponds. Bare-breasted beauties were bathing in crystal clean mountain streams. Sculptured bamboo groves waved in the refreshing morning sea breeze. A lone farmer guided his beasts of burden through rich coal-black soil. Fruit vendors and street merchants set up their wares in order to catch the morning rush hour foot traffic. The old battered and rusty corrugated metal stalls that line the village roads look utterly sublime in their bright-orange hues. It was dawn in Bali, and despite the benign enchantment, the first leg's home stretch lay before us, beckoning us on.

We unfortunately had to endure nonstop music as we drove. At the moment the sun squinted at us from the distant mountains, the bus driver slapped an Indonesian disco tape into the deck and blasted it as we inched our way into Denpasar. We tried not to let the noise cast a shadow on the light. We also had a disheartening string of bad luck during our first few hours that morning on the island of Bali. Serious car trouble. And we had to alter our means of transportation on no less than five separate occasions before high noon, as we raced through hidden corners of the fascinating island in six incredibly mesmerizing hours. Our first *bemo* ride. A localized version of LAX's *Super Shuttle*, *bemo's* are tight and cramped, have bad exhaust and non-existent brakes. But we found that the *bemos* were just too sluggish for our fast-paced existence as we attempted our ascent up a rugged volcanic mountain range. Its stop gap replacement, a freshly painted *Volkswagen* van, broke down on several occasions. Despite Andy's repeated efforts to suck gas through clogged-up fuel lines, we left our driver and flagged down another *bemo*. (I have this picture of Andy convulsing along the side of a dusty Balinese road taped to my computer as I write.) Poetic justice for the snakes he made me wear earlier in the race I thought? I was catching up now. Chalmers-1, Valvur-2! I myself, attempted to help by doing what I always do when I have car trouble, call *AAA*. Wouldn't ya just know it, my membership card had expired.

After a brief ride on board an ox cart, we hitch-hiked a ride with three friendly, overweight German tourists in an aging, and now severely cramped *Suzuki* jeep. Somehow, we're absolutely convinced that it was a *Grace of God Production*, we came across a vacant taxicab high atop a rugged mountain road en route to the designated volcano recreation area near emerald-colored Lake Batur. We convinced the sleeping, bewildered, and all together reluctant driver, into taking us to the rest of our Balinese destinations.

Achieving full momentum with a set of decent wheels, we visited the Spirits of the Sea *Tanah Lot Temple*. Tanah Lot is the Balinese pagoda-like version of France's Atlantic coast *Mont St. Michel*. And one of the best places on this planet to witness an awe-inspiring romantic sunset…trust me! Then off to *Tampaksiring Temple*. A fountain of youth-type shrine where ancient mythology runs as deep as its crystal clear blue water. I dipped my spiritual member into the cool holy waters. We sped onward to visit the artistic woodcarving center in the peaceful village of Mas to purchase a specific ceremonial Rama dance mask. The not so wild monkey forests of mountainous Ubud was next on our list, followed by the thick vegetation-covered and camouflaged 11th Century cliff-carved tombs of *Gunung Kawi*. We finally paid our spiritual respects to the appointed Mother Temple of Bali, named *Pura Besakih*.

Also known as *Pur Panataran Agung*, this sprawling mysterious complex of over thirty temples is where spiritual pilgrims beseech the gods for holy purification. It is located to the east of the simmering 3,142 meter high Mt. Agung. One of three active volcanoes: Mt. Batur and Mt. Batuka are the others on this relatively small two thousand square mile island. It was here that we donned our specially purchased, color coordinated sarongs and blessed *saputs* (temple sashes), procured in Yoyga's hectic marketplace a day earlier, for a brief tour of the holy site. We chilled out for a few minutes with the Hindu worshipers.

It was just after 2 p.m. on Thursday, when we checked into the magnificently beautiful *Tjampuhan* Hotel perched on a gorge overlooking a deep river valley, after six full nonstop days on the road, for an unquestionably well deserved respite. Ubud village is located in the highlands, some thirty miles north of Denpasar. This was the designated finish for the first leg of JB's bizarre souvenir-collecting marathon. We immediately eye-balled the incomplete and unofficial scoreboard in the hotel's outdoor lobby, and discovered, to our absolute amazement, that we weren't the first Human*Race* team to have arrived in Ubud!

In fact, there were no less than four other teams there before us! Uncertainty and astonishment filled our now overwhelmed, overwrought and exhausted brains. *Psycho-sclerois* I think they refer to it as, the hardening of the mind. "How could this be?" Andy queried. "Were we that slow?" I countered in complete amazement. "How could the others have possibly gone as fast as we had?"

Our egos now severely bruised, our collective pride painfully battered, and our bodies badly road weary and limp from sheer exhaustion, environmental exposure and pangs of malnutrition, we were both much too haggard to worry about such mystifyingly vague uncertainties as our place in the race. Life would go on.

Toute suite we headed for our beautiful, scented and exotically decorated thatched roof cottage, but not before falling into the refreshingly cool swimming pool with all of our clothing on. They were kind of smelly and rancid by now and needed a good washing in the worst way! A luxurious long hot shower followed by an altogether appetizing and nourishing lobster and king prawn dinner at nearby *Murni's*. It was here that we tentatively pondered our fate as we downed a dozen or so icy cold imported Mexican beers. We were now fully primed to *siesta*. Unconsciousness was our next Human*Race* destination.

And so with our mosquito nets tightly in place encircling our cool and comfortable white sheeted beds, we listened to the soothing reverberations of the wind chimes playing in tune with the steady natural rhythm of the geckos mating call in the background. Silence never sounded so loud. We were soon lullabied into a deep sleep, like babes in the woods.

The name Bali, translated from *Bebali,* (offering to the Gods) which goes a long way to explaining why it feels like such a spiritual place to begin with. People seem to be attracted to things they don't entirely understand as part of our rather humbling human condition. Like men and women for instance. It is said that there are over thirty thousand temples and holy shrines on this sacred island. That's one temple for every eighty people! You simply can't escape religion in Bali. Statues ward off evil spirits at every intersection. Daily offerings are seen lying in the streets in front of small shops and one-room homes. Ceremonies abound, for the living, for the dead, for the young, for the old, for the married, for the newborns. It is believed that through their expressed applications of cultural spiritualism; that by making their temporal physical worlds as beautiful as possible, they guarantee for themselves, their non-physical souls at least, a safe and glorious journey to their even more serene and eternally everlasting afterlife. How can you quarrel with that kind of spiritual logic; cherishing life's temporal beauty now to better enjoy the beauty of the spiritual afterlife! One way or the other, I reckon, you can't miss. It's definitely a user-friendly religion. As America's modern day guru of myth and philosophy, Joseph Campbell so eloquently states, "Follow your bliss." To which, I might humbly add *this ain't no dress rehearsal.*

In the extensive literature available on Bali, it is said that all of the islands' 2.5 million men, women and children are artists of some kind. In fact, it is assumed that everyone is artistically predisposed for they don't even have a word in their ancient vocabulary for an individual artist, with a capital A. It's apparently in their genes. It's in their nurturing as well. Everybody is creative here, whether by engaging in clay sculpture or wood-carving, being a painter, dancer, puppeteer, costume designer, musician, poet or a reader of ancient stories. Their combination of reverence towards individual spiritual happiness and communal cultural ritual, makes Bali a stimulating and enriching environment where exotic exhibitions of art and religious expression alike, are pleasantly interwoven into every aspect of daily life. From the perfectly manicured terraced rice paddies to the tenuously perched mountain top volcanic villages. The preservation of ancient, unceasing Balinese traditions alongside its more relatively contemporary taboo free Hindu *dharma* exoticism influences, constitute an extremely intriguing cultural *melange*, one offering the best of both worlds filled with shared communal ceremonial observances and more profoundly personal and private expressions of spiritualism.

Great Islands
Balearic Islands
Bali
Canary Islands
Capri
Crete
Galapagos
Gilligan's Island
Iceland
Maui
Phuket
San Juan Islands
Santorini
Society Islands
Vancouver Island

We slept peacefully in our special room numbered: *River One Down*. The spotted and brightly colored gecko, we called him George, holed up in our rather rustic bathroom, became our live and let live friend. He ate all the bugs in our hut! Up and ready to order breakfast, we banged on our special *chukulu*, a hollowed-out wooden carving of a man with his penis extended, to order room service! Our private house boy immediately materialized after hearing the echoing *chukulu* thud. Fresh papaya juice, piping hot Java, mixed tropical fruits and banana pancakes were served to us on the verandah overlooking the Tjanmpuhan River gorge. We could see naked beauties bathing in the stream down below.

We engaged our *twentysomething* house boy in some idle chit-chat and learned his whole life story in a few minutes. He had crushed another man's skull with a rock he said without much emotion. The man died, he went on. Something about a fight over his long time girlfriend. His adversary was a despised foreigner, from the neighboring island of Java, he explained. I tried not to look overly concerned by the voluntary manslaughter charges that he was confessing to. Although shocked by his matter-of-fact admission of guilt, we allowed the conversation to ramble on to more conventional subjects. Like night security systems and cattle prods. "Women," I reassured him, "they'll do that to you every time! Don't feel too bad." And it didn't seem that he did!

Despite the uncertain future over our security, one awakens daily amidst the titillating beauty and heartwarming serenity that makes this an enchanting tropical island, a mind-boggling *Shangri-La*. It's almost too good to be true. Ubud is a particularly tranquil, warm, charming and colorful, artistic community that has come to epitomize the "true Bali experience." Snakes and all! It is in fact, the very cultural heart of Bali. One is constantly surrounded by the pleasing radiance of art, their culture and their lush tropical landscapes, and especially the people themselves. This extraordinary combination truly makes this place a special corner of the world. You feel like you're a thousand-and-one miles away from the hectic hustle and bustle of busy downtown Denpasar, or the sunny and sandy beach tourist-plagued resort communities of Kuta and Sanur.

Despite our restful surroundings we were both somewhat restless. A syndrome one suffers from when traveling at near break-neck speeds across remote and exotic lands. It's hard to slow down. You've got to see everything possible in the limited amount of time you're given. This type of traveling is not for the faint of heart. We also knew that we had to eventually venture out from our cozy and comfortable home-away-from-home in Ubud village and witness for ourselves the changing nature of Bali. There is trouble in paradise, so we went shopping for Buddha's…

Tourism and technology, the twin scourges of the 20th Century, have wreaked certain havoc on this island community. In 1988 alone, over five-hundred thousand members of the species, known collectively throughout the world as *homo touristicus*, patronized this comparatively tiny and relatively isolated enclave. Bali, located within Indonesian's so-called Spice Islands chain, is often referred to as the jewel of the Indonesian archipelago. Well, parts of this shinning jewel is approaching rhinestone status. It is under attack by commercial airline and ocean cruise ship assaults which have fostered numerous unfavorable urban-like consequences, such as: debasing adolescent prostitution, petty property crimes, crass consumerism, rapid-paced environmental decay, drug addiction, widespread social dislocation, ruinous economic inflation and debilitating underemployment to name just a few ills. All the evils of bright lights, big city life have been brought to a tropical getaway.

I have listened to stories from those folks who called themselves travelers back in the 1960's and they speak of a Bali which we did not find. I suppose all good things change once everybody knows about it. The sure result of the *Loving it to Death Syndrome* (LDS). I imagine modern Maui must seem an abomination to people who have been going there for years. Mass tourism is unforgiving and progress certainly is a bitch!

Yet, at the same time, this primarily Western-based infusion of tourist dollars has served to strengthen some of the more exotic theatrical displays of native Balinese spiritual rituals. In fact, many village children attend special dance and music academies, funded by the local island tourist association, where they learn both the art of performing their highly refined ceremonial rites and the extraordinary history behind the exquisite choreography of their many cultural dances. Cultural reinforcement does take place, albeit commercially facilitated, by the popular steel and cement high-rise hotels that line the fashionable beach communities.

Having a commercial ocean-front resort, is a tad ironic for the serene people of Bali, because the average resident disdains the warm crystal clear blue ocean waters surrounding their tropical island paradise. They don't like to go in the water! And who can blame them? Many of the islands landlubbing citizens' friends and relatives alike have met with an abrupt, never-to-be-heard-from-again, untimely death. Or worse, for these are a highly imaginative legend producing people, some have survived the sea's perils with a great horror story to tell. Between the deadly seasonal monsoons, stepping on lethal stonefish, succumbing to quicksand-like riptides, ferocious eels, nasty sea snake encounters, plundering Filipino pirates, the odd roaming great white shark, nausea inducing open sewage pollution, and the ever present toxic blue-banded octopus, the highly inviting tropical waters off the Bali coastline are, at times, not such a friendly place to play. And as a result, you rarely ever see the locals frolicking in the warm sun, soft sand and soothing surf.

Despite this local preoccupation with the terrors of the sea, there are two types of radically different tourists that come to Bali to be by the water. First you have the sleep-on-the-beach set that frequents the sandy Sanur Beach resort area. This recently over developed *Miamized* resort community has vanquished most of the local native flavor, in favor of the wholly alien *West is best, bigger is better* and *money does buy happiness* trilogy of American philosophies embedded in the so-called good life. All three of which are the pivotal themes of our materially-based, Western celebrity-oriented cultural consciousness, epitomized by junk food, junk bonds and junk mail. The local residents have learned from this mode of conspicuous consumption gone awry, and social evolution being what it is, they have adapted accordingly. Strolling hawkers and tin stalls line the beach area, each offering their own versions of the typical tourist crap; trophies for the folks back home. Their simple, yet self-sustaining expectations of material welfare get so unconsciously skewed by this continuous contact with wealthy tourists, that their future lives can't help but be somewhat frustrated by these unobtainable dreams of excess. Para-sailing, speed boats, sparkling jewelry, scuba gear, jet-skiing, expensive fruity drinks poolside, hundred-dollar dinners and the like, are all alien materialistic philosophies injected into their ancient and spiritual island traditions. Other cultures have called it spiritual pollution! At times the scenes that one encounters strolling the beaches of this area, borders on the vulgar. The slow, but steady encroachment of the modern world on traditional, yet civilized societies, is never a pretty sight. You can't help but become ashamed that you too are but another commercial tourist corrupting these innocents abroad.

The second group of tourists that visit Bali, come on well packaged trips to Kuta beach. Kuta beach is so crazy, crowded and commercialized, it's extremely difficult to say anything good about it. This time however, it's not the ugly Americans' fault. This grotesque tourist ghetto is for the most part, a creation of the rowdy Australian *banzai* beach surfer class. Walking through this area is eye-opening. It's future shock Balinese style. The hordes that attack Kuta mostly hang around a sprawling commercial complex of endless merchandising stalls, gaudy neon-colored surfer shops, belching diesel trucks, chic native fashion boutiques, gaudy jewelry stores, bootleg record stores, mangy packs of dogs, fast talking pimps, screaming motorcycles, and scores of urine smelling *Bingtang Beer* honky-tonk video bars. I counted at least a dozen discos in this small area alone. Food emporiums serve *Vegemite* sandwiches, pizza slices and spicy tacos. Hundreds of wandering hutless hawkers, freelancing on either side of the dusty and muddy streets, pester you endlessly as you pass by. It's really remarkable how all the shit they sell in tourist stalls looks the same, no matter where in the world you roam. There must be a single factory in Tijuana or maybe even on the West Bank, that makes all these hopelessly worthless and tacky tourist trinkets. The marketing vice-president merely stamps different made-to-order destination labels on them: *Made in Tangiers, Venice Beach, Product of Thailand, Acapulco, Made in Kathmandu or Piccadilly Circus*, take your pick, but it's always the exact same crap.

Kuta's an extremely trendy locale where gnarly native print T-shirts, rad traditionally made sandals and boss bright-neon swim wear can be purchased at exorbitantly high righteous prices, dude! The Aussie dude ethic here is simple: *Surf. Get drunk. Get high. Get laid.* Your basic adolescent teenage Ft. Lauderdale spring-break rape and pillage-like mentality. A pioneer take-no-prisoners manifest destiny type of attitude. But here it takes on unmistakable ethnic, racial and holier-then-thou colonial overtones. We're certain that decades ago this was a low-cost peaceful utopia for the *faux* Bohemian jet-set culture. But now pleas-ure-seeking Aussies in the hunt for great waves, cheap beer and even cheaper babes, have simply taken over. It's now nothing more than a beach front holiday camp for extremely rowdy and horny surfers. Damn the legendary rich native island flavor and distinctly elegant primitive culture. Damn the local tranquillity and sensational beauty of the exotic flora and fauna. Damn the unearthly mystical spirits and the communal religious spiritualism. Utopia lost once again. Gaudy displays of Western affluence gone amok. The paradise of Eden gone forever. Innocence lost.

Another sad case of *White Man's Burden* revisited. Where the belief exists that modernization is wanted, and inevitable. But to modernize actually is a euphemism to eradicate the ancient local culture. Bali has joined the international jet-set circuit and now must compete for tourist dollars with the likes of Miami, Cancun, St. Tropez, Acapulco, Mykonos, Rio, Ibiza and Waikiki. A sad commentary on progress I say.

As for the jam packed beach itself, well, there's another problem. Bali has over a thousand miles of beautiful sandy white pristine beaches where you can isolate yourself without too much difficulty. Unfortunately, you can't even contemplate restful relaxation on densely commercialized Kuta beach. Don't even attempt it. Do not pass the beach entrance sign. Do not pay the beach fee. Do not go to Kuta beach, period! Despite it's well-earned reputation as one of the best places in the world to experience the sunset, (It rivals, in my humble opinion, the daily sunset exhibitions at Key West's *Mallory Square*, *Rick's Place* west of Montego Bay, Santorini's glorious *caldera* perch and Kato Beach on the Island of Phuket's nightly light show.) the continuous barrage of beach hucksters pestering anything that moves is just beyond compare.

Every thirty seconds on average, and we timed it, graduates of the Indonesian Marketing Academy poll your every need. The local entrepreneurs in the booming global souvenir biz call out, "Allo sir…Do you want a nice and soft massage sir?" "Very cheap!" she adds. "Allo mister…Do you want an icy cold drink?" "I have some excellent magic mushrooms today!" "Are you from Sydney…or Melbourne?" one particularly inquisitive seller asks. "Oh, America!" he happily learns, "USA Number One!" Again and again you continually answer by a simple shaking of the head or with a more terse "NO!" It seems not to deter these folks in the least. And they won't let you ignore them either. With bright delightful smiles and no sense of bitterness or contempt whatsoever on their part for your continuous snappy refusals, they calmly and happily reply, "Okay sir, maybe later. Have a nice day." And they mean it! Then they just stroll away en route to their next victim only yards away. "Allo lady…"

Now, this is fun for a few minutes. A little different even. God knows you don't get this kind of service at the local mall or on Main Street, but…over the course of an hour or so at Kuta beach, these pointless introductions, unwanted sales pitches, and subsequent in vain rejections on your part takes place hundreds of times under the scorching hot sun. Sunglasses, kites, plastic toys, colorful blankets, someone's sister, straw beachmats, high-fashion hats, potent hashish, styrofoam boogie boards and surfboards, designer watches, silver jewelry, somebody else's brother, rubber flip-flops, sodas in a rainbow of flavors, an assortment of international beers, sensual massages, magic mushrooms, and cheap shares of *Microsoft* common stocks, (Without broker's commission and fees of course!) are offered you at every turn. Even the highly dignified and somewhat pious Balinese, have come to develop their own version of the American street-hustler or scam artist. If the translation was correct, the term was *Bohong*.

We sat and had a few beers at *Madie Warung's Bar and Grill*. The street scene got very ugly. We began to swat away street urchins as fast as the flies attacking chips and salsa…"Enough is enough," we eventually screamed, succumbing to a severe bout of manic-nirvana. We quickly located a *bemo* driver who immediately tried to sell us some marijuana for our tiresome and bouncy journey back to the subdued hillside town of Ubud. We wiped the *KS* (Kuta Stink!) from our weary brows. Damn the sunset we thought, we'll get a brief glimpse of the equally astounding sunrise over the perfectly sculptured rice paddies along Tjampuhan Ridge in the morning.

A full moon ruled the clear black sky. Fireflies buzzed our verandah and bull-frogs and geckos sang Bob Marley tunes on this sweltering humid evening. Even the birds were fooled by the brightness of the full moon. The natives seemed restless. But then again, it was just another Saturday night in Ubudtown. After drinking heavily in the shade of the *Royal Lotus Pond Temple* at the *Lotus Cafe*, we were ready for a good time. We had been fortunate enough to procure a couple of prized invitations to local Prince Putra's famous village palace along the Ayung River gorge for an exotic evening of delicious vittles and traditional Balinese entertainment. We were told that this was merely a dress rehearsal for an even larger village wedding celebration due to take place the following morning. We found ourselves active participants in what was to be an evening of evil spirit chasing. A small donation for the arts, was requested from us upon entrance. A hundred thousand Indonesian *rupiah* note seemed a suitably small price to pay for all the wine, women and song we could fancy.

Well okay, so the beer was luke-warm and the women turned out to be a couple of nuns conducting missionary work from the Seattle, Washington region. The rhythmical music and sensual dance was beautiful and wondrous nonetheless. We were downshifting into a more relaxed mode.

The portly Prince of Ubud turned out to be a pleasantly literate fellow and a charming host. This only goes to highlight the utter importance of selecting your parents wisely in the Third World. It's a precariously fine line between a destiny of sheer ecstasy or one of total deprivation. Our host had picked out a King and Queen as his parents. We were impressed! I felt a little bad for the overly-excited Prince Putra when the semi-cooked BBQed suckling pig unceremoniously squealed as he carefully carved into it to open the banquet's festivities. A little too rare I thought! Somewhat embarrassed, but without missing a beat, the regal Prince gestured the slightly uncooked sow back to the barbecue spit for some culinary fine-tuning as he pronounced, "A little too rare!" to his hungry yet entertained commoner guests. Despite the early glitch, the evening turned out to be a wonderful feast of traditional fare intermixed with polite, almost royal dare I say it, conversation.

Among the other Westerners though, it was mostly your all too typical white-liberal guilt-ridden exchange verging on Green political dialogue. The new fashionable battle for the liberals without a cause. The invited guests debated such lofty ideas as: the ozone layer and the saving of the world's precious rainforests, restoration ecology and debt-for-nature swaps, and even the recent mysterious resurgence of the *El Nino* weather conditions. All of which was peppered with a heavy accent on pre-fab New Age-speak. "Nothing like traveling ten thousand miles to meet Americans and discuss the op-ed pages of the *Washington Post*!" I sarcastically noted to Andy. So we figured, what the hell, and unmercifully dropped an intellectual cluster bomb on all of them. It exploded each of their pointy little heads like a full bottle of whiskey smashing on concrete. Walking away from the dinner table I casually asked a rhetorical question that had been personally bothering me for sometime, "Wouldn't a nuclear winter solve our global warming problems?"

I for one, have never gotten used to this bonding phenomenon. I like to call it the *Away from Home Syndrome* (AHS). A situation where native countrymen, *species americanus* in this particular case, who have nothing remotely in common with each other, save their present geographic coordinates, seem to bond and fondly reminisce about home while being away from home! Talk about the *grass is always greener* cliché. I also, rightly or wrongly, explain it as a rather complex by-product of the modern day Age of Leisure and 20th Century Affluence mixed together with an unhealthy, need-to-know dose of need-to-know information anxiety. Not to be snobbish or unfriendly, but I was in remote Bali, Indonesia, and wanted to enjoy the local flavor. This down home shallow Des Moines, Iowa, idle banter just wouldn't do. So, immediately following the smorgasbord buffet, Andy and I quickly moved off to the *ad hoc* Hall of Fine Arts within the sprawling palace grounds for some live entertainment.

For the next three hours we sat absolutely mesmerized, as we watched an extraordinary display of masked *Wayang Wong* dancing. Consisting of exotically made-up pre-pubescent village girls moving sensually in absolute synchronization to the hypnotic rhythm of the *gamelan* orchestra, it was truly something out of the pages of *National Geographic*, and we had front row seats. Eighty-five local musicians, all playing an unusual array of percussion instruments, made up the boys-in-the-band. This enchanting ballet of sorts, performed together with the voiceless orchestra's haunting and discordant tunes was immediately followed by a marvelous ancient shadow puppet play called *Wayang Kulit*. It wasn't as breathtaking as the mega-production Broadway hit *Les Miserables*, but the story line, based on Javanese tales of traditional boy-meets-girl and good-over-evil themes with the hero being a beloved Hindu prince, was both emotionally touching and culturally interesting.

After all this consumption of tasty food, exotic art and rich culture, we clearly needed to chill out. We were to leave Bali at dawns early light from *Ngurah Rai* International Airport, and that thought was becoming more and more depressing. So we wandered along moonlit rice paddy paths in the general direction of our rustic hotel. The night air was damp with the fragrances of sweet acacia and jasmine. We came across a relatively quiet Australian watering hole called the *Beggar's Bush*. "But of course, how very creative." Andy mocked. "Certainly not a local haunt I'm guessing," I furthered as we quickly ordered a round. We played a toss-the-ring-on-a-bullhorn for an hour or so with a few ice cold *Fosters* lagers, but after listening to some mushroomed-out transplanted Malibuddhist surfer dude utter something about what he called "trans-cultural empathy" from the bottom of his beer glass, we opted for the peaceful serenity of our hillside *Tjampuhan Hotel* for an earnest attempt at a good nights sleep. I dreamt that I was chasing fireflies into the wee hours of the night.

The following morning rumors about us spread once again like wildfire through the ranks of our fellow Human*Race* contestants. We took it as a clue to our perceived corrupting influence when it was said, by wholly unnamed and anonymous sources of course, that our late night shenanigans included skinny-dipping under the moonlight at midnight and twisting by the pool to the soulful sounds of *Simply Red*, and just generally carrying on till the water buffalo came home. With of all people, now get this, the nuns from Washington state! "Preposterous!" Andy told a fellow contestant. "Utterly sacrilegious!" we immediately pronounced. How ridiculous it all seemed. Rumors, innuendo, and baseless stories. Another urban legend thrust out into the world. None of which we would of course either confirm or deny, thus letting our outlaw reputations grow more insidious as each day passed. Attitude is an important element, an ally if you will, in any long distance race. You need that psychological edge. And let it be known, we had our fair share of attitude.

Dawn Came Early, and Other Stupid Opening Lines...

Oh those wonderful jasmine-scented Singapore Girls! It's true what they say about them too. Warm smiles that make your heart melt, non-stop feminine grace and exceedingly exceptional service that puts Buckingham Palace's royal house keeping staff on report. Still, it wasn't a lot of fun knowing that we were about to embark on yet another mind-numbing thirteen hour airplane ride.

Let's think about air travel for a minute. You sit strapped in a small uncomfortable chair in a silver metallic tube, built by a company that submitted the lowest-bid, some 35,000 feet above sea level and maneuver through the turbulent atmosphere at speeds in excess of 500 mph while eating shitty re-constituted microwaved food, breathing stale unhealthful recycled air and being subjected to bad movies that failed horribly at the box office. Never my idea of a good time. Hell, the only time I rejoice is when we successfully get off the runway and then when we're safely back on it. And yet somehow air travel still retains an aura of genteel luxury. I simply don't get it. But I guess it's better than being tossed around on a ship for a few weeks. Or riding elephants across the Indian sub-continent!

Andy of course, having been a flight attendant for a number of years, tends to agree with my assessment. There were times, he says, when he worked flights in the US that he swore most of the passengers had shoes on for the first time. At least traveling in and out of the developing countries you expected people to look a little rougher. He remembered

his first flight, a 24 hour marathon from New York to Tokyo via San
Francisco, Hawaii and Wake Island in 1957 aboard a *Pan Am* Boeing
Stratocruiser. Talk about mind numbing! He remembered the passengers were all well dressed throughout the flight and the service on board
was luxurious.

But I regress. Before we could continue the great race, we had a six-hour
layover in Singapore, during which we had to endure yet another of JB's
prolonged press conference/dinner parties. It was held in our honor at
the grandiose *Holiday Inn Park View* on Orchard Road, and it was an
elegantly tasteful and civil affair. A sumptuous eight course gourmet
Asian meal was served. Our table hostess was a perky young upwardly
mobile Singaporean Chinese woman named, Dinger. She sure was too!
I'm sure we asked her about the origin of her name, but the answer was
lost among the beers and various dishes. Expect the unexpected in
names while traveling. You learn to listen intently and get the name correct, at least phonetically, on the first run through of intros.

Dinger was a gregarious, friendly and extremely humorous women in
her early twenties. She thoughtfully explained that she was working her
way up the hotel's corporate ladder. Rather effectively too, she added with
a wink of her eye. But alas, the poor girl, never could quite fathom the
explicit objective of our peculiar Human*Race* expedition. It became
embarrassing after a while to continually attempt to rationalize to people,
that we had paid a princely sum of money to travel around-the-world in
burlesque game show fashion. Tonight however, the burden of anxiety-
ridden justification was mellowed by a continuous flow of cold imported
Irish ale and deliciously prepared Peking Duck.

It went downhill from there. For the next few hours, we watched an
extravaganza of buffoonery that we eventually became desensitized to
during our *Whirled Tour 1989.*

Let's see, not only were we told that we were officially positioned
in fifth place after the Human*Race*'s Southeast Asian segment,
through some application of accounting and scoring principles that

to this day completely escapes our collective sixteen years worth of higher education, but, to add insult to injury, we encountered the following tormenting tourist tribulations: yet another bar bill padded beyond belief; a way-too-talkative taxicab driver that just had to know our personal positions on the recent Zsa Zsa Gabor-Beverly Hills cop-slapping trial (Or was it the Jim and Tammy Faye Bakker televanglism fraud trail? I still get those two *National Enquirer*-like sagas confused!), while stuck in LA-like gridlock en route to the airport; a totally indifferent ticket agent as we elbowed for airspace at Singapore's ultra-modern *Changi* International Airport; multiple misplaced transcontinental airline reservations; and finally, being unceremoniously informed that we were being bumped into cramped seats in the smoking section! This was followed by a so-called "temporary mechanical delay" (Due, we're certain, to a malfunctioning idiot light flashing in the cockpit that, after an hour of nervous finger-tapping by the flight's engineer, eventually burnt itself out without anyone ever actually knowing what was wrong with the plane in the first place!); and last but not least, a world famous Chicago O'Hare Airport special, an "air traffic control delay" of about thirty-five minutes. I guess there was just too much traffic over the Indian Ocean for that sole worker on the Island of Mauritius to handle!? Don't you just hate when that happens! It really was an ugly chain of events to be sure.

It's not letting relatively trivial things like these get to you when you're traveling, read: racing the globe, that separates the casual once-a-year vacationers from the truly professional travel junkies. And we are serious travel junkies. Just knowing that those warm, colorfully dressed and almond-eyed Singapore Girls were waiting to accommodate our every whim, helped us grin and bear our on-the-road ordeal a little better.

But oh those Singapore Girls! With a quick fix of double vodkas, neat thank you very much, and a steaming hot towel, the lissome creatures of comfort helped us relax knowing full well that our impending destination was Cairo. "Wonderful!" Andy lamented, "From the Jewel of the Orient to the cultural trash heap of history."

Now I know Andy was either too full, tired, drunk or dazed to make such a cogent statement like that normally. It must have been that little blue pill that I gave him earlier. He asked me what it was, I just smiled and said, "Never mind. Trust me, you'll like it." "But I've been drinking?!" he tried to tell me. "Even better," I replied. He's a lightweight and has tried to avoid taking pills since he was given one a long time ago at a concert at Winterland in an atmosphere of peace and love and woke up a few days later wearing a dress in a cheap motel. It wasn't the motel that he minded so much, it was the dress, he said, "Too short!" He didn't quite have the legs for it I guessed.

But I digress once more. We were headed for Cairo. I was actually excited because I was finally going to see the Sphinx. I fell asleep, rather quickly I might add too, humming: *See the pyramids along the Nile..*.

Even as our 747 made its final approach into Cairo, heavenly Bali, despite all its unpredictable and quaint periodic power outages, was still lingering in our collective consciousness'. Hell, we had even left behind our colorful sarongs and temple sashes at the Ubud village dry cleaners. I guess we'd just have to return someday to that inspiring, sultry and bewitching island. In the meantime, we'll hang on to our claim checks and hope that old Zulu inspired proverb is true, that "...*those who meet, will meet again.*"

Needless to say, filthy, seemingly war-ravaged Cairo was not our preferred city to hang out in. In the back of our minds, Andy and I had been hoping for an immediate State Department terrorist bulletin. A cautionary travel advisory or two prohibiting us altogether from entering Egypt. No public announcement, civilian warning or cautionary report of public notice came from any unnamed high-ranking US Government officials. This urban purgatory clearly wasn't on par with other enticing destinations like Paris, Goa, Dubrovnik or even Orlando for that matter! Yet somehow we had to stomach literally and figuratively the pending reality of this swelling metropolis on the verge of fundamentalist anarchy. Despite the negative thoughts we harbored for our destination, we were determined not to suffer any psychosomatic symptoms of the much dreaded *Economy Class Syndrome*, (ECS) for all you acronym buffs, where stuffy jam-packed (The average coach seat is only 21 inches wide and offers all six foot two inches of me a whole 31 inches of leg room!) back of the *airbus*-type conditions that lead the occasional weary traveler to develop symptoms of quivering and quaking in quiet desperation due to tight congested quarters and bad food. Thank you Singapore Girls, we love each and every one of you.

Dawn came early, as I regained consciousness from my *Halcion* induced nine-hour sleep just prior to our Egyptian touchdown. Well at least I thought it was dawn. The time bandits had stolen yet another day from us. The only thing I vaguely remember about the flight, was a conversation I may, or may not have had. Andy can't help me with this at all. Apparently I was spinning a prayer wheel as an aggressive Japanese investment banker was trying to sell me on the spurious idea of time-share condos on the Southern coast of New Guinea as we flew over the Arabian Peninsula. I don't know that I bought into his heavy-handed sales pitch, but I was missing a personal check drawn on my *Nugan-Hand/B.C.C.I.* bank account when we landed. Andy claims it was just another one of my surreal semi-lucid dreams. Maybe so, but funnier things have happen to me at high altitudes. I made a note to myself to call my neighborhood banker ASAP.

Through the supposedly soundproof aircraft cabin walls I heard the crying wails of the Mullahs, above the roar of aging MIG's taking off on training flights and incessant honking of automobile horns, known affectionately here as the Egyptian brake pedal. Cairo, the City of a Thousand Minarets was awaiting us. Our globe-trekking misadventures were about to undergo a dramatic change in venues, and the Middle East was now our center stage.

Jumhuriyat Misr al-Arabiya, known to most of us simply as Egypt, is a visually haunting place. Land of the hustle, hassle and the hard sell. They seem to have perfected it over the last five to six thousand years of civilization. It was once known as the agricultural bread basket of the known world. Now they can't even feed their own fifty-one million citizens. Depending, for the most part, on billions in foreign aid every year from their oil rich Muslim Godfathers and massive American dollars-for-peace bribe money. As weighty geopolitical and socio-economic classifications go, Egypt classifies as an NDC or *Newly Declining Country*.

As for Cairo itself, the so-called *City of the Victorious* and *Mother of the World*, well, this seething, breathing monster of a city, estimated to have over sixteen million residents, the largest city by far on the African Continent, can best be understood via a simple game of word-association: streets-dusty, sounds-horns, cuisine-*Pharaoh's Revenge*, hospitality-evil eye, order-chaos, climate-hot 'n' smoggy, architecture-collapsing, culture-old, very old, cold beer-N/A, women-black veils. Does any of this mean anything to you? Maybe not. But even New York City seems to have its shit together compared with this place.

By now, you can no doubt sense the depth of my displeasure at being brought here, yet another Third World megalopolis! It was an ugly picture imprinted in our mind's eye. Magical, tropical and serene Bali still lingered in our thoughts, yet we were racing and had places to go and silly tasks to perform. The race continued. It was time for work. And the distant future pleasures of clean streets, tasty cuisine, pretty women and modern Europe, next stop on our Human*Race* itinerary, would just have to wait. It was time for deferred, versus instant gratification. And time as they say, whoever they are, for the tough to get going. And so we did. The bell for Round Two had just rung. We were standing erect though somewhat bloodied. It was a rude awakening. The campaign for North Africa was beginning and we were the Allies, the contemporary desert rats if you will and the arid wasteland Egypt lay before us.

We promptly checked into our provisional peaceful oasis in Cairo, the well-worn but safe *Ramses Hilton Hotel*. A dreary modern concrete mono-lith overlooking the so-called *Sixth of October Bridge*. Built, oddly enough, in remembrance of an especially demoralizing Egyptian *defeat* at the hands of the fierce Israeli Defense Forces in 1973. The hotel was located alongside the greenish-brown banks of the tirelessly flowing River Nile. The Ramses would become our sanctuary as we came and went into and out of the searing hot desert and through the chaotically congested and dusty streets of downtown Cairo for the next three or four days. From here we mapped out our strategy for the taking of Egypt.

Not unlike Nazi-era German Field Marshall Erwin Rommel, the self-proclaimed Desert Fox, Andy and I had decided to conquer the outer reaches of this sparse and dusty land of the ancient Pharaoh's, namely, the port city of Alexandria. From there we'd head for the Upper Nile city of Luxor, before tackling the bigger problems located here in the capital city of Cairo. Our tactics were simple: travel light, be extremely efficient (In a notoriously inefficient country with over five thousand years of bureaucratic procedures!), don't drink any water, or eat any food for that matter, and get the hell out of here as quickly as we possi-bly could. In Egypt, like in most of the African Continent, one should always remember that traveling per se, is not an adventure, but more of a glorious achievement.

We sprinted across town to the perennially busy and tattered *Ramsis* Train Station to chart out our intended course. As we performed our now customary and ritualistic *train schedule boogaloo*, we booked to Alexandria, but wished that it could have been to Clarksville, and also got tickets for the night train to Luxor.

While on the scenically unimpressive three hour train ride north to this Nile Delta region, we encountered a rather witty nuclear physicist from Cairo University. The two of us had a stimulating and varied conversation with this professor-engineer-civil servant on the future of Egypt in gen-eral, but touched on some provocatively controversial and heady topics such as: the overly zealous Muslim Brotherhood and Iranian-inspired Islamic fundamentalists; America's role in the sometimes on-again but most times off-again Middle Eastern peace process; the economic policies of Egyptian President Hosni Mubarak; OPEC's oil-pricing strategies; and the more contentious issue surrounding the world's most intractable dispute, the Israeli-Palestinian conflict.

As he enthusiastically lectured us about Egypt's bright social and economic future, I peered out the window of our speeding air conditioned train. As far as I could see, we were on a train going back in time. I couldn't help but sense the utter timelessness of this ancient civilization. The ancient Egyptians are the proud inventors of crude irrigation techniques and the ox-drawn plow. Not much had changed in their technological development it seemed. But the sights I was seeing, were nonetheless pleasing to the eye.

Smooth sailing *feluccas*, like dancers, maneuvered in ballet-like tandem up and down the River Nile, truly a natural wonder all to itself. Field laborers called *fellahis*, patiently tended their small plots of land and green pastures as their ancestors must have done some four thousand years ago. Occasionally camel caravans carried colorfully dressed Bedouin nomads from one desert oasis to another. Overloaded donkeys trotted along bearing their owner's produce to village markets. Sluggish beasts of burden plowed their master's rich fields of black soil. We saw goats tethered on the rooftops of clay and straw built homes. Snowy white egrets flew in flocks just over the tree lines. Black-haired and smiling shepherd boys tended to their small flocks of goats and sheep.

Natural Wonders of the World
Victoria Falls, Zimbabwe
Aurora Borealis/Northern Lights
Mt. Everest, China-Nepal
Great Barrier Reef, Australia

Grand Canyon, USA
Particutin Volcano, Mexico
Rio Harbor, Brazil

As we continued to roll along, we talked about the prospective future of nuclear energy, food processors, data processors and word processors. It didn't seem right. It just didn't fit into the enigmatic ancient reality of the Egypt we were now experiencing. Of course I understood most of the issues relating to nuclear energy and God knows I've become an expert of sorts about processed everything. We got the big picture as the intelligent, yet seemingly overly optimistic professor painted it. I just didn't comprehend how any of this contemporary 20th Century technology, no matter how misapplied, could be integrated into this chronically backward civilization. Egypt may indeed have been the *Cradle of Civilization* a few millennia ago, but nowadays they required the constant attention of a paternalistic baby-sitter. The all too apparent irony of it was just too much to think about.

We arrived in time for an early lunch at the Moorish looking *Masr* Train Station in fabulous downtown Alexandria. The city is named after Alexander the Great, the famous teenage-warrior who conquered and modernized this easy going seaport town around 330 BCE, not *Before Cable Either* this time but *Before Current Era* for the MTV crowd! Rumor has it that a lot of hanky-panky took place in this historic party town. The Palm Beach of Egypt. It's falsely known as the Egyptian Riviera. No sandy white beaches saturated with suntanned topless Egyptian or Libyan goddesses here. Alexander, the illustrious Greek from Macedonia, had a harem of desert-raised lovelies that tended to his every whim while planning his military campaigns East via the famous Silk Route.

This rather illustrious historical era was followed a couple hundred years later by the ever sensual Queen Cleopatra, who celebrated by frolicking on Caesar's Imperial barge with that manic-depressive Roman playboy, Marc Anthony. If our boring *Western Civ* lectures are true, and the historic tradition of Imperial Roman rulers playing with matches would seem to support it, then legend has it that a tremendous inferno set by jealousy-prone Julius Caesar burned down half the town. Close to two thousand years after that infamous scandal, the young Corsican General Napoleon Bonaparte, delighted in the local ladies whilst sunning his bloated body on the beaches prior to attending to his various European military obsessions. Actually, Napoleon's *Grande Armee* later lost in a stinging defeat to the Egyptians, but the debacle went mostly unnoticed in the French press back home.

Today Alexandria is a shabby, overpopulated and decaying historic relic of a city with but a few redeeming qualities aside from the breezy fresh Mediterranean sea air.

Our sole complication during our fleeting two hour *grande* tour of the ancient city was that of our taxicab driver. He hoodwinked us completely. Since every taxi driver in the world retorts to a tourists standard trademark query of "Do you speak English?" with the corresponding yet equally deceptively pat "Yes!" answer, it's important to test and understand the true nature of his, or her, English-speaking capabilities by throwing out a fool-proof follow-up question. Our tough cross-examining *$64,000 Question* on this particularly bright n' sunny day in Egypt was, "Do you think it's going to snow today?" To which he quickly responded, "No way sir!" in a most insistent manner.

Sold on his top-notch linguistic talents we pointed out our four specific Human*Race* destinations on a tourist map we had secured earlier. He nodded declaring that there was "No problem boss!" as we successfully haggled and negotiated for a more favorable price for his services. Easy enough. Or so we thought…

While driving along the breezy *Mediterranean Coast Highway* (MCH) en route to King Farouks famous *El-Montazah Palace* on the far eastern side of this long and narrow port city, we noticed that Mohammed (Everybody seemed to be named either Mohammed after the great

Islamic prophet, or Abdul, after Kareem Abdul Jabbar, the great Los Angeles *Laker* legend!?) was driving at a rather leisurely speed as he pointed out scenic coastal vistas to us. At first we smiled in appreciation looking first left then right, nodding our heads thinking he was giving us the quick nickel tour of Alexandria. We then began to nervously check our watches. Andy looked at me, and I at him with eyebrows raised. We grew progressively more anxious to his sluggish snails pace. The click of plastic worry beads broke the uncomfortable silence. "We are in a race," our communications officer Andy informed him over and over again. "Have to catch a train in two hours back to Cairo," I further insisted. He nodded and snickered, "Yes sir, no problem. I understand."

It finally dawned on us that when an Egyptian says no problem it's our version of saying "The checks in the mail." Or the Hollywood rendition of "Let's do lunch."

To make a long and extremely frustrating story short, Mohammed thought he was on the time clock and was getting paid by the hour as opposed to completing his chauffeuring duties quickly for a sizable gratuity. He couldn't understand English, or American for that matter, and he reckoned that we were trying to fleece him out of some hard earned extra money to feed and clothe his harem for his extra time on the job. He thought that the slower he went the more money he was going to make.

His economic logic was inescapably correct under normal labor union negotiations and his evil-eye expressions became more and more threatening to us. He was a husky, muscular and menacing looking man with one long jet-black eyebrow, who we're certain had many longshoremen-type co-conspirators in this coastal city. We on the other hand, knew only a single balding middle-aged professor from the local university who, we were speculating wildly now, hadn't boxed professionally in years. Growing increasingly emotional and more animated by the minute, as our collective understanding of his now distinctive Arabic dialect increased in direct proportion to his inflamed temper, we sought linguistic counseling from an elderly clerk at a nearby hotel. After a drawn-out and rather boisterous debate, a Middle Eastern peace initiative was brought forth on our parts.

"*Aday? Aday?*" (How much? How much?) we asked him over and over again. Finally we got our answer. Our wallets in hand and our checkbooks out, Mohammed successfully negotiated for all the *shekels, dineros, pesos* and pounds he wanted. He got what he wanted, then, *ipso facto*, he instantly became our new best friend in Alexandria. Smothering us with brotherly affection and showing us pictures of his two children and his brother's three girls whose freshman year's in college we had apparently just financed. "Just get us out of here, and quickly!" was our only demand.

A microcosm for sure of the entire Arab-Israeli conflict we thought. They don't speak the same language and can't even decide on what the actual issues are; no one talks directly to the other party. It's always through paid intermediaries. More importantly, both sides don't want to give up anything. They both want to have their cake and eat it too. At any rate, this is what we happy travelers designate as a *friendly assault* in the Third World, as opposed to just a plain assault, where they simply steal your money at gun or knife-point. But we had to let it be. No arrests would be made here. No official Egyptian Tourist Authority complaint form Nos. 67-T567-091 would be filed in triplicate against Mohammed. No reprisal air strikes would be launched. No hostages would be taken. No eye for an eye vengeance attacks. We fully capitulated to the inescapable reality of our predicament and rolled with the punches. We would make our afternoon train schedule yet. Though a tad poorer. But first there was the matter of our scavenges.

At *Pompeii's Pillar*, a giant eighty-eight foot-high red granite phallus-like column made for Emperor Diocletian in the Third Century in gratitude for *not* massacring the rebellious towns people no less, we ran into further trouble. We were reprimanded in several languages for taking pictures without a properly obtained tourist photography permit, it cost $5 at a nearby phonebooth looking wooden hut. That was an original one we thought. The scammers were getting scammed on. Apparently signs were posted all around the historic structure's perimeter. Unfortunately, our college hieroglyphic deciphering capabilities had suffered from severe disuse and were a tad rusty. In fact, the scam was nothing more than that old rich tourist shake-down gimmick. This kind of shit happens in the Third World. Hell, it happens in Little Havana, Harlem, South Boston, the Westside of Chicago and Watts for that matter. But we don't travel through any of those equally exotic destinations.

We didn't want the prolonged aggravation of having to explain our side of the story to the harmless, but much dreaded Egyptian Tourist Police. Nor did we want to risk the chance of being unjustly declared *persona non grata* by an offended Egyptian Ministry of Internal Affairs official. Or have to deal with the nasty Senate Sub-Committee on Foreign Relations upon our return back home. Nevertheless, we had to deal with the matter, as effectively and quickly as possible. So, despite breaking the spirit, if not the letter of the American *Foreign Corrupt Practices Act*, the situation was ultimately easy to settle. Nothing that a little *baksheesh* couldn't solve.

Baksheesh is Arabic for a bribe. An extortionist's *payoff*, a *lubricant*, a *kickback*, a *present, payola, palm greasing, gratuity, hush money, sop*, a *finder's fee, hongo*, a *brokerage commission*, or whatever you want to call it. Some Western diplomats commonly refer to it as official development aid and goodwill gestures. There's a word for it in every language on earth and usually begins when you hear the words "I think this is going to be difficult!?" We classified it as just another friendly assault in Alexandria. The cost of doing business in this part of the world. Trickle down economics at work. "Besides," I told Andy, "It was tax deductible."

We were both beginning to understand this brow-beating hold-up mentality all too well. Three strikes and you're out as they say. It was time to get out of Dodge. And quickly! We wanted out of Alexandria. But first things first.

We sprinted up and down the over two-hundred marble steps leading through the stuffy and dark *Kom al-Shokafa Catacombs*. Quickly, we found all of our historic clues in a little known gem, the excellent *Greco-Roman Museum* before returning to the relative safety of the train station. That was an especially ungratifying two hours spent in the day-and-life-of two now fully committed cultural terrorists running recklessly through the grimy ancient streets of Alexandria. As Julius Caesar deftly said a few thousand years ago, "*Veni, Vidi, Vici!*"

We barely made it to the station and settled back comfortably into our seats with a *Coke* and a smile for the one-hundred and twenty mile, three hour ride back south to Cairo. We were being hesitantly pushed back further into the interior of Egypt, by the not so subtle breezes of the famed wickedly dry Sirocco desert winds.

While riding the rails up 'n down the sacred Nile River Valley from the Delta to the Dam, we took to song writing in a vain attempt to lift our somewhat depressed spirits in this increasingly bleak environment. It was also a feeble attempt to ease the boredom we were now feeling. It was day eleven on the road and we were reaching out for the familiar. I personally wanted to answer my voicemail and play phone tag at the office. After about a fortnight on the road with people using abacuses to calculate our bar bills, I longed to check with my broker to see just how badly my stock portfolio was doing. I wanted to *Fed-Ex* something to somebody somewhere. I wanted to edit my Filofax and fax in my luncheon order to my favorite Italian restaurant, *Ca'Brea* in LA. I wanted to check in and know if I was actually missed at the office, or if indeed I was nothing more than just another cog in the big wheel of commerce? I yearned to pay my bills, even on time for a refreshing change of pace. I wanted to do lunch on Montana Avenue. I even wanted my MTV.

Music seems to bring you back home somehow. It allows you to connect with your familiar, though distant surroundings. So we wrote a few songs, ditties actually, in a fruitless attempt to ease our now extremely travel weary souls.

Our first tune took but a few minutes to pen as Andy, always the musical phrase turner, pulled this one totally out of the hat. Catching his sense of rhythm, we both hummed and sang aloud. The song was a natural, and it rolled off our tongues effortlessly. Entitled "*The Third World Blues*," it kind of goes like this:

I got dusty shoes,
I'm reading yesterday's news.
Don't look now but my food just moved!
Oh Lord, I got the Third World Blues.

I'm livin' in a cheap hotel,
Haven't been eatin' well.
Had my fill of spectacular views,
Oh Lord, I got the Third World Blues.

Can't check my credit rating,
Cuz there's no call waiting.
Life on the road, ain't no Italian wedding!
Oh Lord, I got the Third World Blues.

Things are looking up,
We've stopped throwing up.
But there's no A/C on the back of this bus!
Oh Lord, I got the Third World Blues.
Oh Lord, we got the Third World Blues....

Crude, but to the point we thought, as we rattled along the railroad tracks on a seemingly endless journey. OK, Lennon and McCartney we're not! After this rather dubious attempt to write the definitive traveling song, *a la* Willie Nelson's *"On the Road Again,"* we opted for a different angle. So in the tradition of those Hope and Crosby *"On the Road to…"* high-jinx travel adventure flicks, we penned this rather appropriate, but as of yet untitled road tune:

> We're Valvur and Chalmers
> and we're on the road.
> From Hong Kong to Cairo
> we're always at home.
> Our bags were too heavy
> so we lightened our load.
> We're Chalmers and Valvur
> and we're on the road.
>
> From Bali to Paris
> we're searching out bones.
> We're hungry and tired
> but the beers are all cold.
> Temples, Cathedrals
> they all look the same.
> One more photo with natives
> and we'll go insane.
> So remember,
> he's Valvur and he's Chalmers
> and we're on the road…

Okay, so the supporting actress role of Heddy Lamar is open and still not cast as of this writing. But hey babe, we've got casting agents and the Lonely Hearts Dating Service working on it. Hope and Crosby we're not. More similarities can be drawn from Dustin Hoffman and Warren Beatty in their legendary bomb-of-the-decade *"Ishtar"* we were summarily informed. Clearly we were getting extremely silly. "Don't call us, we'll call you," said the recording execs of Columbia Record's obscure *Desert Island Discs* travel music division. Not in the least bit discouraged, someday you can find these songs along with a few of our other favorite travel melodies, like: *"Do You Know The Way To Bucharest?" "Has Anybody Seen My Luggage?" "I Left My Stomach In Seoul Korea."* Along with our personal favs of *"Warm Beer, Cold Stares"* and *"My Body's in Coach, but My Brain's First Class!"* And finally, the completely irrepressible number *"We'll Sign For It Blues."* All will be included on our self-produced greatest hits travel music package distributed on *K-Tel* records and tapes. Available on our own *Grace of God Productions* label soon.

Around 7 p.m. that same evening, we boarded the infamous *Nile Express's* First Class compartment bound for Luxor on an indecisive note. We considered the possibility that the overland bus may have indeed been the quicker mode of transportation, but opted for the first time to surrender time, in favor of riding in relative comfort on board the train. It was a big trade off that we felt we could afford: speed versus leisurely comfort.

Luxor, or *Thebes* as the Greeks called it, was the capital city of the United Kingdom of Upper and Lower Egypt around 1550 BCE. Today it is a thriving, tourist filled city located across the River Nile from this ancient City of the Dead. This was where the Valley of the Kings and Queens, Tomb of the Nobles, *Medinet Habu* and *Temple of Hatshepsut*, among other archeological discoveries, had been unearthed. This kind of antiquity was almost too much to comprehend. Our minds and bodies were growing increasingly weary by the day…nay, by the hour!…for we were still in fact biochronologically on *Indonesian Daylight Savings Mountain Time*. One of those modern jet-age time-space anomalies. OK, we were suffering from jet lag!

The scientific study of the malady of jet lag is a budding new discipline of sorts. It's a 20th Century growth industry where government R & D grants are easy to obtain; probably because all the Members of Congress get effected by it when they take their official global junkets.

Sometimes referred to as the *Transmeridional Malaise* (TM), but by whom I don't really know? TM is the by-product of a combination of negative traveling factors: moderate to severe dehydration, an altered and chaotic dietary intake, road stress and a discombobulated natural body clock. Several Human*Racers* had succumbed to the sickness at various times during the trip. Some had even bowed out. We, on the other hand, were members of the walking wounded majority. We were constantly monitoring our physical conditions and we continually found ourselves licking our wounds along the way. A catnap here. A *Snickers* bar there. My personal prescription is to drink lots of bottled water (Non-carbonated whenever possible.), eat high protein foods and subject yourself to well timed periodic bursts of high-intensity fluorescent lighting. It works wonders.

Unfortunately for us, we didn't fully realize that our leisurely ride south would turn out to be another spine-numbing fourteen hour trek to our southern Libyan Desert destination. "Great!" I grumbled. Andy wasn't thrilled about the prospect either. But grin and bear it we did. We thought that we could catch up on some much needed shut eye and be daisy fresh for our appointment with ancient history in the morning. The up-side of this late night desert excursion was that we were planning a sunrise power breakfast with the famous boy-king, His Royal Highness Tutankhamen.

We had hoped for an uneventful night train ride through the hot desert wilderness, as we danced along the edge of the Nile. What we got was an episode straight out of the "*Outer Limits*" TV series.

Several other competing teams were also utilizing the same sleep-on-the-move strategy that we were, and we had a Human*Race* rally of sorts on the train. But let's not get too carried away we thought, no cold brew or salty pretzels on this express train. Just the same, we were without a doubt pleased to see some familiar faces. Crazy man, Mitchell Daniels, a San Francisco-based executive assistant to the CEO of *ESPRIT*, along with his always up-beat partner, Kevin Erdman, a Northern California cameraman, were making the midnight run with us. As were two of our more ferocious competitors, known collectively as the Del Ray Boys, William La Tulip and Mike Shalan of Del Ray, Florida. Always grinning Mike Cerre, the producer and owner of the Sausalito, California-based *Globe TV* production company was also on board with his always impeccably dressed partner-in-crime, Sir Kenneth Crutchlow. Crutchlow, a British subject now living in Santa Rosa, California who is an importer by profession, is not really a Knight of the British Empire. But a *Sir* in my book under any circumstances.

Media disinformation, ancient lore and legend has it, that in the early Sixties, Crutchlow, a stout and hearty English gentlemen along with an Australian chum of his, were downing a few pints of lager at their favorite West End London local. Their loud and meandering discussion turned in the direction of adventure and travel. As Kenneth cavalierly recalls it, a dare backed up with a side bet was made. As in most gentlemen's agreements, a lone pint of lager was the total extent of the wager. The preposterous deed they had agreed to challenge each other to was something a tad more noteworthy however. Crutchlow and his drinking buddy had decided to compete *mano-a-mano* in a hitch-hiking race around the world. The rules were simple: No begging, no borrowing and positively no flying. They wholly depended on the kindness of strangers. And to make it more of a challenge, they could only take the money they had in their respective pockets at the time of the bet. Ten pounds sterling for Crutchlow, and just twenty US dollars for his counterpart. About even. To document their global exploits, they had mutually decided on three global check points: the foreign desks of the *San Francisco Chronicle* and the *Sydney Star*, and finally, the *King's Head Pub* they were now sitting in. The bartender witnessed the informal agreement.

We sat and listened to Crutchlow for hours en route to our ancient destination as he weaved his seamless tale of the ultimate travel adventure. From secretly stowing away in Captains' quarters on board ocean-going vessels, to frequent liaisons with Cold War-era spies and arms dealers, and occasional run-ins with tribal chieftains, his adventure story got wackier as it developed. At times it reminded me of a cross between several Hollywood movie epics, one directed by John Huston entitled "*The Man Who Would Be King*," the zany comedy called "*The Great Race*," and finally, of course "*Around the World in 80 Days*."

Crutchlow eventually won this race in the end, actually completing his fantastic voyage in a mere ninety-four days. His Australian buddy gave up somewhere in central Asia, the pint of ale was sadly never collected and very little fanfare was accorded Crutchlow for his extraordinary global feat. But the sheer audacity of his mind boggling triumph warranted a knighting in our books. Maybe even a Presidential Commendation. If Frank Sinatra got one, why not Crutchlow? And so we saluted Sir Kenneth Crutchlow, dressed in his typically British traveling attire: a blue wool pinstriped suit, brown-plaid deerstalker cap, and ever present black umbrella. All a true English gentlemen really requires! We toasted him with a spot of luke warm watered-down tea as we rock 'n' rolled onward into the night.

DATELINE: CAIRO, EGYPT: (REUTERS)

Six male Americans competing in an
around-the-world scavenger-hunt race
died early this morning in a blazing
inferno on board an express train en
route to Luxor. Thirty-one others also
perished in the apparent electrical fire
as authorities from a nearby desert
oasis tried in vain to rescue the
passengers in a remote section of the
Sahara desert. Their charred bodies will
be flown to New York City in order to
complete the race. Funeral arrangements
are pending.

This was how our obits would have read, in a single two-inch col-
umn-filler piece buried somewhere no doubt on the bottom of page
thirty-three adjacent to a *Chanel No. 5* perfume ad in the *New York
Times*, if it wasn't for some quick thinking, and some even quicker
maneuvering.

As if by psychic-tuning in anticipation of a prophetic cataclysm waiting
to happen, Andy and I awoke together only split-seconds before a blinding bolt-out-of-the-blue fireball shattered the otherwise peaceful calm
of the black desert night. We had just crossed over a bridge at about four
a.m., when the indoor pyrotechnics display started. We quickly leaped
out of our seats as heavy smoke started to bellow from the galley area of
our compartment. The train slowed almost immediately, it's brakes
screaming in the still night air. The acrid smell of burning electrical
wires filled the air. Between us, we attempted to awaken the other race
contestants and fellow passengers in the now darkened car. We
painstakingly made our way to the sole exit to discover that that's where
the blazing fire was located. We somehow shoved the door open. Fresh
air filled the cabin fanning the flames as we hastily jumped off the now
dead-in-its-tracks train to the relative safety of the cool desert. An *8mm
SONY* videocamera was carefully tossed to me as I assisted other passengers jumping from the fiery cabin. "Lights! Camera! Action!" ordered
Cerre, the ever-ready veteran news anchorman. The camera was on,
focused and recording our all too real crisis live and in living color. Sam
Donaldson of *ABC's "PrimeTime Live"* would have admired the presence
of mind.

The next few minutes unfolded into a frenzy of activity with train
engineers ranting and raving, an international array of panicking passengers and curious wayfaring Bedouins gathered near the perilous
scene to watch the inferno.

As quickly as the fire's peril was evaluated, our potentially aborted
transportation situation was also noted with immediate concern. We
were physically safe from the fire, but now stranded in the middle of the

desert. So after everybody was safe and out of harms way, Crutchlow, ever steady in his dark blue pinstriped suit, crawled on all fours with me under the adjoining railway cars as we dashed into the night backtracking towards the trestle. Amidst the camels, donkeys, goats and hollering locals we spotted a group of cars. We immediately flagged down a rather uncertain-looking Arab driving a vintage wood-paneled station wagon. A flurry of hand gestures and broken English dialogue ensued. Money was waved in the air. Lots of money as I remember! Within a few minutes of awakening in the middle of a potentially lethal train fire we had successfully secured alternative transportation to Luxor.

Hey, are we pros, or what!?

With the electrical fire now fully extinguished and after a protracted discourse between the enraged conductor and the equally teed-off engineer as to just who's fault the fire had been, the *Nile Express* was restarted. Because our car was right behind that of the two engines, no electrical current flowed back to us nor the other cars to the rear of us. The journey would be continued, but without the benefit of cabin lights. There was no air conditioning on board this train, so we wouldn't be missing that. We opted to stay on board the train, so we gave our hastily discovered and would-be taxi driver some *baksheesh*, thus insuring his deep personal concern and cooperation. It was now approaching dawn, and after an hour or so delay, the ordeal ended as quickly as it had started. We were on our way, albeit ever-so-slowly, south. Our *crisis de jour* was over. We had survived yet another unrehearsed, wholly spontaneous Human*Race* event. We would live to embellish this tale to our grandchildren.

We finally staggered off our train into the hot blazing sun at the rather run-down Luxor train station around eight in the morning. Two full hours behind schedule, that was already two full hours too slow to begin with. We had lost a lot of time by taking the express train. In retrospect, the bus was clearly the way to go. But memories of our interminable road trip across Java pushed us over the edge of clear thought.

Prior to leaving for Luxor we had advance booked a flight aboard hijack-prone *EgyptAir* for our return trip back to Cairo. The flight however, the only one available on that day, was due to depart at 1:30 p.m. That would give us roughly four hours max to cover more than five thousand years of ancient Egyptian history! Our dream of one day visiting the celebrated *Valley of the Kings*, arguably the most famous and historic archeological site in all of the world, was about to come true, in the configuration of a hurried tourist nightmare.

Stepping off the train we hastily elbowed our way past dozens of touts: potential guides, antiquities dealers, Arabic translators, taxi drivers and beggars, as we quickly made our way to the East bank of the now severely polluted River Nile. Here we negotiated a ride on board a dangerously overcrowded ferry across to the famous West bank *necropolis*. As we crossed this sacred river, I noticed the incredible source of life that it brings to the people of Egypt. The palm-fringed banks of the cloudy gray river was, and will continue to be, their very center of gravity. Aside from water to drink, they depended on their Mother river for: transportation, water for crops, nourishment for their beasts of burden, recreation and mystery, washing their clothes, floating prophets in baskets and God only knows what else.

Looking up and down the river I saw teams of sailboats bobbing and weaving, giant green lily pads floating along with the currents, and groups of small children bathing in the water, as the bright morning sun's intensity made my eyes squint in submission. I saw large floating river boats line the shore here at Luxor, a testament to another sort of existence that the river brings its people. These huge multi-decked ships carry people on overnight cruises to Aswan and other historic places. They provide dinner cruises and even serve as backdrops for Agatha Christie mysteries. And despite the hardships of this old country, ever since I was a little boy, I've romantically entertained traveling the Nile from the Alexandra on the Mediterranean to Khartoum in the Sudan.

It might happen someday, but not anytime soon. That's another trip to take in the *Big Book of Life*.

Upon docking we immediately arranged for a driver to both chauffeur us to our required Human*Race* destinations, as well as expedite our way through the unmerciful maze of unscrupulous touts, tacky tourist traps and Tutless temples. It was a bizarre delight to be sure. Almost surreal. To be at long last passing through the very neighborhood where Egypt's Old Kingdom (3,500-2,200 BCE), Middle Kingdom (2,100-1,800 BCE) and New Kingdom's (1,600-1,000 BCE) were the very focus of civilization, art and culture to the known world. Don't tell the Chinese that though! We were visiting the world's greatest open outdoor museum.

Across the river lies Qurna, a small dusty village that has sprouted to house the workers who make their living on tourist *marks, lira, yen* and dollars. Kind of like an ancient Orlando adjacent to this Disneyworld of the Dead.

Like any world-class museum, tourists from around the world crowded to see these must-see sights. Like religious pilgrims swarming to their holy grounds, these modern day Egyptologists can be just as fanatical in their single-minded pursuit for a viewing angle, a mummy postcard, King Tut T-shirt and of course, a photo-op with the proper backdrop.

I personally hold Thomas Cook to blame for the whole shameless state of contemporary corporate international tourism. This devout Baptist missionary is to blame because he's the one who created the very first, and now infamous *package tour* way back in 1863. He's the culprit that created all these unrelenting commercial centers in every corner of the world. He used history, architecture and alien customs to market and sell the whole white middle-class society on becoming a collective gang of roving tourists. Today I call it *Cynical Tourism* because now nothing is left to chance: pre-packaged tour operators send 747 after 747 and mega-cruise ships to exotic locales with restored historical districts, mass-produced art colonies, pre-fabricated art festivals, processed character and food stuffs from wherever you want. These travel agents provide fake surrogate experiences in synthetic re-cre-ations, facsimile experiences at fantastic prices. It seems that today it's possible to go almost anywhere and learn almost nothing and feel like you never actually left home!?

(Readers please note that there is another version of our below visit to Tut's Tomb you are about to read. Something having to do with a "Not Open" sign and a *Swiss Army* knife!? But on the advice of counsel and the suggestions of some high ranking State Department officials, I'm sticking with this sanitized version of the story!)

As we drove toward our first scavenge, we passed several children riding donkeys next to the black asphalt highways that stretched off towards the bleak yellowy-gray limestone hills in the distant horizon. This arid and dusty place was somehow devoid of landscape. We arrived at our first destination of the day in the *Valley of the Kings*, the famous *Tomb of Tutankhamen*. Revealed not by its numerous signposts, but by the throngs of Euro-styled *Volvo* and *Mercedes Benz* tour buses parked in perfect parallel formation, row upon row outside its barbed wire entrance. It looked like the Pentagon's parking lot. We parked in the pink Sphinx area. We heard mostly German and French accents as we queued up to view King Tut's early-Nile decorated burial chamber. Oddly enough, Tut's tomb is actually the smallest of the sixty-two pharaoh tombs in the surrounding area, but overwhelmingly the most popular. Dying young has its up-side. Due no doubt to the professional services of a high-priced Beverly Hills publicity agent!

When we began our descent into the hallowed tomb itself, I couldn't help but experience a sense of drama. Just as I'm sure the renowned archeologist, Howard Carter, felt in 1922 when he too initially ventured into this celestial chamber of the nineteen year old boy-king. We strolled past the richly painted walls of Tut's burial place with about a hundred other visitors in tow, all *oohing* and *aahing* in unison as we marched forward in an orderly single file. Andy and I were consciously careful not to breath too heavily or sweat too profusely; over six gallons of perspiration a day help oxidize and gnaw away the ancient chamber's unique wall frescoes we were informed! In the ongoing battle between antiquities preservationists and the local chamber of commerce, the latter win$ out every time. They are very efficient here, and if you believe me, and you have no reason not to, we were in and out of King Tut's final resting place and afterlife playroom, in less than two minutes.

We left Tut's chamber humming the immortal words of Peggy Lee's hit single, "...*is that all there is*?" We didn't know whether to laugh or cry. Years of anticipation. Months of preparation. Weeks of traveling. We had risked our bloody lives! We had spent a small fortune, and we were in and out in two minutes! The only thing I could think of was Steve Martin's farcical *"Saturday Night Live"* sketch in which he sings his now famous King Tut song: *"Funky Tut, got a condo made of stona...buried with a donkey. King Tut..."* Boy, were we jaded or what! Disappointment *numero uno* on a morning of world-class disappointments had just taken place.

Our skewed expectations and dreamy hopes, like those you get from an over-hyped up movie, or before the *Super Bowl*, had unfortunately preceded us into the Valley of the Kings. We had fallen victim to sensationalized press releases. Disappointment seemed to be the order of the day, as our morning, chock-full of ancient historical experiences, was simply no match for our many years worth of built up expectations.

It was hard to explain why we were continually disappointed by the magnificent and historical sights we were seeing. Perhaps it was the heat of the blazing desert sun oppressively pounding down on us? Maybe it was the hundreds, no make that thousands, of camera-toting tourists clamoring about, that somehow perverted our perceptions? Or, maybe it was the severe jetlag we were suffering from or the hectic pace of the race itself, now entering its second full week? Perhaps we had read too much about this historical spot and our expectations had completely usurped reality? Were we irrevocably over-exposed? It could happen, we reassured ourselves, as we briefly surveyed our shattered perspective of ancient history. Or, maybe we had succumbed to the mysterious, dreaded and legendary curse of Tut? Or, maybe these ancient artifacts and run down monuments of a bygone era were just too old, too worn down, too sterile and too far removed from their ancient historical context, that their grandeur just couldn't be fully appreciated? Some scholars spend lifetimes uncovering the mysterious secrets of these ancient architectural wonders and extinct spiritual myths, yet after one short hour we could barely wait to leave. Windsurfing in the Pacific blue near the County Line was on my mind.

We couldn't put a finger on the answer to our unsatisfied cultural appetite as we continued to view, entirely unimpressed by this time, the *Tombs of Seti I, Ramses IX* and *Amenhotep II*, and a miscellaneous assortment of other dead-as-a-doornail and buried with their livestock Pharaohs. All incredible chronicles of human vanity to be sure. From there, we went to the *Valley of the Queens*, which houses numerous other tombs of the ancient Pharaoh's families and the magnificently carved three-tiered granite *Deir el Bahri* or the *Mortuary Temple of Queen Hatshepsut*. Here lay the famous bearded Queen. The ladder temple was built by the twenty year old queen while she was still barely a sophomore in college. Ole Miss I think it was. Or maybe Upper Nile State?

Still, staring at this huge edifice carved out of a mountain you gain a little respect for those ancient cultures. It also made me wonder. If they were so evolved all those thousands of years ago and have now declined, what does that portend for western civilization with all our TV's, faxes and satellites? Will people someday stare in wonder at the twin towers of the World Trade Center in New York and wonder what happened to all the Yuppies? Or worse, will Las Vegas be the truly remarkable archeological site of the next millennium?

Here, in what turned out to be a moment of comic relief, we had to have our picture taken in full Arab attire, on what JB termed a four legged animal. We chased down a particularly slow moving dish-water gray donkey grazing on rocks, cigarette butts, *Big Mac* containers and broken *Coke* bottles about a half mile from the busy Temple. I wish I could share with you the queer look on the donkey's face when we approached him with an offer he simply could not refuse. The situation was utterly absurd and priceless at the same time. Two howling, bleary-eyed tourists changing clothes in the middle of the desert putting on full Arab head gear and a colorful red and white *galabiya* while trying to keep the donkey from running away. We were now also suffering from, along with numerous other road weary maladies, *Ethnic Costume Dementia*. Couldn't blame the little four-legged beast in the least for trying to escape. We would've run from us too. Finally, we mounted the poor wobbly-legged guy. It was fortunately over very quickly.

We continued our tasks in a trance-like fashion moving from tomb to tomb, temple to temple, passing tourist after tourist. But the smell from the donkey episode was always lingering nearby. We couldn't escape our past transgressions.

We thought we had seen everything there was to see, when we happened to read a little blurb that interested us. According to Egypt's Ministry of Culture, there were over two thousand ancient tombs, monuments, pyramids, colossi and obelisks still unearthed through-out Egypt. And despite their careful and highly labor-intensive methods, the article went on to say that it would take, on average, two full years to appropriately unearth these soon-to-be future tourist attractions. We decided to see those tombs we missed the first time around in Egypt with the rest of the yet to be uncovered ones on a future trip. Far off into the future we hoped. Like in the year 3,989! We figured that another two thousand years of mystery just might add some luster to their distinction. Couldn't hurt. But, then again, if we are to believe the recent theory of an ideologically impaired and wholly misguided former State Department official that the so-called "*End of History*" was upon us, then maybe we'll miss out on the other tombs altogether. Oh well, we did our best. Can't see and do everything your first time around the world. Or can you?

Sent out into Egypt to rediscover the mysteries of the past and having a little difficulty, we sought the enthusiastic assistance of a visiting Syracuse University specialist, Ray Johnson, Ph.D. We had been having trouble at the *Temple of Luxor* interpreting one of JB's scavenges. We had been asked to take a photo of ourselves with the statue of *Osiris*. But, without the benefit of a guide book, we couldn't find where it was supposed to be in the courtyard of Ramses II's temple. We spent a long time guessing until we queried Ray, who was busy copying hieroglyphics from a particularly battered column. "A wild goose chase!" he quickly explained in no uncertain terms. We'd been had. Although some other HumanRace contestants later claimed to have found it! We chatted for a while, as Ray explained the history and architectural styles of this well preserved temple, which ranged from the New Kingdom to Roman eras. We then said our good-byes and were finally on our way to our last stop before returning to the chaos of Cairo.

We truly enjoyed our leisurely stroll through the sumptuous *Temple of Karnak*. We passed row upon row of ram-headed sphinx, in what must have been a truly majestic facility thousands of years ago. The complex was immensely huge and we savored the cool relief it offered us from the high noon sun as we hid in the shade of its hundreds of colossal 80 foot columns, sucking down lukewarm sodas sold to us by a couple of enterprising little boys. Dedicated to the then mighty god Amun, the enclosed *Great Hypostyle Hall* is large enough to accommodate the famous medieval cathedral of *Notre Dame* in Paris. The *Karnak Temple* covers about sixty square acres and is considered the greatest monument built at the height of Thebes' ancient glory. Our excursion into the Lower Kingdom's history was now complete. Time to catch a plane out of here.

Quotes From A Street Vendor

"Andy," I asked in a foreboding tone, "Do you have any idea which international airline is most prone to accidents and terrorist incidents in the whole world?" The poor guy looked stunned as he squirmed in his seat. I had pushed his ultra-sensitive safety button. He didn't want to know the answer, cognizant of the fact that his partner, the irrepressible info-junkie that I am, probably read this juicy tidbit somewhere. "No, not *Eastern Airlines!*" I laughed aloud. Then I matter-of-factly informed him, "*EgyptAir!*" Andy sunk low in his seat, inhaling short quick breaths of tobacco-filled air as he struggled to tighten his seat belt. "Thanks a lot," he said. "But did I really need to know that now Bill?" he whimpered with a shaky voice simultaneously searching out the inflight safety card and looking for a phantom cocktail waitress.

I mock Andy, and yet I take great comfort when I fly with him. I know that I have my own personal flight attendant who will get my ass out of the plane no matter what. Besides, he doesn't scare that easily. As I mentioned earlier, he speaks fluent Estonian and German, along with bits of French, Japanese and Bronx. When a high-jacking does happen, he'll just eat his passport and speak with an accent. Meanwhile I'll have to make do on my fractured *Quebecois* French.

We flew back from our ancient history lesson in Luxor on an *EgyptAir* 727, landing in Cairo around 2:30 p.m. We of course made it safely, without major incident or carnage, although Andy may never be the same. We quickly hailed a red *Mercedes Benz* cab into disturbing and haunting downtown Cairo. Once again, the constant din of car horns followed us everywhere. The Cairene's collective mental health must surely suffer severe distress under this habitual blaring of horns. We have concluded that *The Big Honk*, as we came to not so very affectionately refer to Cairo, must indeed be the front runner for the dubious distinction of the noisiest city in the entire world. Between the noise pollution from the endless honking of the horns and the equally bothersome and powerful mega-watt minaret loudspeakers, decibel levels exceed that of Venice Beach's densest boombox/rapper area.

Despite our now aching heads lose gyroscope, our current g.d.t. or *general direction of travel* as they say in these urban desert parts, was toward Cairo's local version of the five thousand year old southern *Thebes* City of the Dead: the *Mausoleum of Qait Bay*. It's a fifteenth-century gray marble and multi-minaret-decorated Mosque whose picture can be found on the back of the filthy Egyptian one pound paper notes, our only clue to what it looked like or its whereabouts. It is unfortunately located in the middle of a rather grim ghetto that is surrounded by acres and acres of vandalized tombs, crypts and gravestones. It is Cairo's version of *Forest Lawn*. I don't want to say it's in a tough area of town but, not even our taxi driver would venture into the maze-like trash-lined streets with us, preferring to stay in the relative safety of his locked and heavily fortified, and no doubt bullet-proof, *Mercedes*. We asked him if it was safe enough to walk through and he kept muttering, "*Insh Allah, Insh Allah!*" (If Allah wills it. If Allah wills it.) We carefully walked away shrugging our shoulders.

Personally, this reflex statement by most Arabs disturbs me. The ringing fate it brings to any difficult yet wholly ponderable question causes me great intellectual dissatisfaction. I guess it hits me heavy and hard in the department of the contentious fate versus free will debate that I still grapple with in my head. "*Insh Allah*" is just so cavalier yet so arrogant at the same time. Andy wasn't in the mood for a theological debate so onward we ventured into the area surrounding *Qait Bay*.

Although pestered a bit by some local street urchins, we emerged unharmed. Our sense of fear was nothing but a collective paranoid optical illusion. Inspired no doubt by horror stories from people who have never really been to Egypt, but nonetheless felt compelled to tell us what's wrong with the place just the same.

From the drab *Qait Bay* we quickly sped to the nearby *Citadel and Muhammed Ali* (Not *that* Muhammed Ali!) Mosque. This 11th Century Byzantine stone fortress, alabaster mosque and complex of Military Museums offers up a stunning vista of sprawling Cairo. On a clear day you might actually recognize specific buildings. Today, however, wasn't one of those days! But, we were able to look down through the blue haze on the necropolis we had just visited. Looking stunned, I scratched my head in disbelief at our foolhardy actions once again. Andy's eyebrows were raised in concerned retrospect.

We then spent twenty whole minutes examining the impressive quarter-of-a-million piece collection at the *Egyptian Museum*. We marveled at the King Tut exhibit, despite having already seen the bus and truck version at the *Los Angeles County Museum* many years ago. Remember Tut-mania? Although time was running short, we briefly glanced at numerous mummies, a prized golden falcon's head, as well as many other archaeological treasures in the dark and cavernous building. Onward we traveled to the *Ramses Wissa Wassef Art Center*, founded by a well meaning patron of the arts to promote art by children. But, after a quick unauthorized and unescorted tour, we came to the conclusion that despite the founders high artistic convictions, the Art Center was nothing more than a scheme to circumvent the Egyptian child-labor laws, if they have any?! We then rushed off to the somewhat rural town of Memphis. Here we sought Elvis's grave at *Graceland*. No, no, I was just testing you to see if you were still geographically with me. At Memphis, Egypt, we photographed a giant marble statue of Ramses II lying down and an alabaster miniature Sphinx. Ramses II seems to be the most revered of all the ancient Pharaohs. His name is everywhere; on the bus station, the train station, the hospital, our hotel, the local cineplex, dozens of *kebob* stands, and of course downtown Cairo's only mini-mall. Ramses II's presence can be felt everywhere mostly due to his long reign of 66 years in office! But more likely due to the fact that the stud sired over 100 children. Most people in Egypt are probably related to him.

Saving the best for last, we arrived at dusk at the famous *Khan el-Khalil* central market. Built in 1382, it is located in front of the even older 10th Century Islamic landmark of *Al Azhar Mosque*. With an estimated twelve thousand shops, *Khan el-Khali* is reputed to be the largest *souk*, a transliteration of the word market, in the Middle East. And we felt that it was our shop-till-we-dropped duty to visit all twelve thousand. Or at least it felt like we had visited all twelve thousand by the time we left the bustling bazaar. Haggling, even for things you have no intention of buying, is expected of you in this ancient Galleria. Here, between the daily sunset and nightfall ritual of *salat* (prayers), we had to find four specific scavenges: the Egyptian pancake house, a silver *cartouche*, a traditional Arab head dress and *galabiya*, and lastly, some perfume from Mohammed Abdel-Sayed Khattab's specialty fragrance shop.

There's absolutely nothing like traipsing through a teeming Arabic marketplace, Persian bazaar or North African *casbah*. The panoply of exotic sights and pungent smells in this exciting cauldron of activity made the senses come alive. Strolling through the narrow alleys you hear insistent bartering and endless sales pitches, softly-spoken gossip and endless invitations to come in and look, all accompanied by a whispered "Mister...for you...special price." It all combines to create a sense of intrigue that makes you feel like you're the lead in some spy movie. We had been to a few of these ancient shopping malls in our past travels: Marrakesh's famous desert marketplace of the *medina*, located next to what they call *Djemaa el-Fna* or the Assembly of the Dead square; and more recently to the seven thousand shop *Kapali Carsi* (Covered Bazaar) of Istanbul, Turkey which, compared to Cairo's *Khan el-Khalil*, seemed like a corner strip mall. These ancient marketplaces put Edmonton's "world's largest shopping mall" claim to shame.

Great Shopping Districts
Barkhor Bazaar, Lhasa, Tibet
Bogyoke Market, Yangon, Burma
Chatuchak Weekend Market, Bangkok
Ciudad del Este, Paraguay
Floating Market at Damnoen Saduak, Bangkok
Grande Marche, N'Djamena, Chad
Gueckedou Market, Ghana
Camden Locks, London
Night Bazaar, Chiang Mai, Thailand
Pike Place Market, Seattle
Temple Street Night Market, Hong Kong
Thamel, Kathmandu
Toledo Street, Naples
Ginza District, Tokyo
Witches Market, La Paz, Bolivia

These places are all a shoppers paradise, where you can purchase almost anything you can dream of. Although the prices usually start out about three to four hundred percent too high, quick and friendly negotiations can usually bring them down to bargain basement prices. On big-ticket items, like colorful rugs and specially made gold and silver jewelry or hand-crafted leather goods, a cup of sweet tea is shared with the proprietor and adds an intimate closeness to the transaction. In the end you'll at least feel like you got a bargain, but of course you never do. So *caveat emptor*! Row after row of goods are for sale, and each maze-like walkway specializes in different things: leather goods down this aisle, handmade Oriental carpets over there, brass and copper down the next alley, ornate silver and gold jewelry, colorful ceramics, onyx and alabaster, perfumes, authentic and *faux* antiques, tin, fine linens and other colorful fabrics, desert fruits, nuts and vegetables, meat and chickens, exotic spices from Zanzibar, and even some hi-tech electronic components from Japan. You name it, they've got it. And cheap too! Be forewarned however, US Customs agents get personally offended if you attempt to import any exotic items that violate America's well-intended *Endangered Species Act.* Watch out for the hippo boots, ostrich feathered hats, leopard and panther furs, anything ivory and anything made from elephant hides.

As I remember it, we walked out of there bags bulging full of regional trinkets and other useless *tchotchkes.* That's the thing about going to a bazaar like this. You agree to buy something when the price reaches a reasonable level, then you think you are being cheap. Nobody's holding a gun to your head! Of course you're in one of the poorest countries in the world, so pretty much whatever you pay is going to seem like a bargain. And at that, you're still probably paying through the nose.

For over 7,000 years, aside from Cleopatra's brief and scandalous two-year reign, Egypt has maintained itself as a male dominated society in almost every aspect. The point is really driven home when you wander around in the *Khan el-Khalil* bazaar. Nowhere are the ancient traditions of this ageless society more adamantly and stubbornly displayed than within its sacred walls of commerce. Centuries-old coffee shops are jam-packed with men playing backgammon and dominoes in cane-backed chairs puffing away on coal-burning hookah water-pipes as the hectic world around them goes by. All the sales people in the market area are men and it is actually difficult to spot women, except for the brightly colored tourists wearing the *DKNY* T-shirts, clearly overwhelmed by the bazaar's madness. Didn't see any "*I Dream of Jeannie*" types in this neighborhood.

It was while traveling here in Egypt, of all the Third World countries we had visited during the Human*Race*, that we were happy to have undergone the numerous pricks of our physician's syringes. Prior to our Fall departure date we had sought out the Atlanta-based *Centers for*

Disease Control for some free up-to-date medical advice. After indulging in a rather lengthy Q & A session with an expert from the so-called *Exotic Disease Desk*, we felt confident that we were fully informed as to all the hideous forms of bacteria afloat in the world. And there are scores to be sure. Now I'm no hypochondriac by a long shot, but I decided to cover all of the bases just to play it safe, based on all the travel warnings I had subjected myself to. And the only way to get that special *International Certificates of Vaccination* was to get the following inoculations prior to departure to protect us from: typhoid, cholera, tetanus, polio, small-pox, malaria, schistosomiasis, sand flies, dengue, yellow, Congo-Crimean hemorrhagic fevers, Chagar's disease, black plague, swine flu, hepatitis type-A, Plasmodium flaciparum bacteria, rabies, Shanghai influenza type-B, diphtheria, mumps, measles, Japanese encephalitis, meningitis, *para*-typhoid (As if the *real* typhoid wasn't bad enough!) dreaded tsetse fly bites, and any and all forms of the always insidious river blindness.

We seemed to be safe from every type of influenza known to man except of course for oft-occurring PMS, the recent outbreak of the Yuppie flu and that newly discovered *Seasonal Affective Disorder* (SAD). Naturally we kept a healthy supply of those wonderful anti-diarrhea *Lomotil* pills on hand for any ugly occasion that could arise within the depths of our blender-like bowels. We never required any medication ourselves, but we were always ready to help out a few of the other contestants who were in less than fine shape on a few occasions. I usually carry a portable *M*A*S*H* unit in my toilet kit. After all, I was pre-med once upon a time. Nuff said. Some in the race referred to us as "*Doctors Without Licenses!*"

I don't mean to imply that Cairo is unhygienic or anything. *But Cairo is as unhygienic as anything!* Even the most conscientious of *World Health Organization* cleanliness experts don't come calling here anymore. Furthermore, any place where livestock are butchered in dirty alleyways, spitting distance from stagnant sewer water, is questionable in our health conscious eyes; having lived for three decades under the watchful protection of the EPA, OSHA, FDA and USDA, among numerous other regulatory acronyms. Any place where their alleged chicken-meat kebobs (Or perhaps maybe they were rat kebobs as I was later told!?) are rotisseried on rusty hangers over the exhaust pipe of a diesel bus is, wholly subjectively speaking of course, suspect in my eyes. And finally, I'm not a wine sophisticate by any means, but any place where their domestic table wine tastes like the Red Sea and their only beer is made in Amman, Jordan, is wholly objectionable to my highly-refined Canadian brewery weaned taste buds. Most uncivilized stuff it was. You can tell you're in an Islamic country that is dancing on the fine line between an outright ban on alcohol and the need to cater to hard currency carrying tourists. They have beer and wine, but their hearts just aren't in it. In fact, it might be in direct violation of certain Geneva protocols against inhumanity towards tourists we thought. But alas, we were safe from any and all living or unliving, foreign or domestic, micro-organisms, bacteria, fungi and toxic-laced fluids that could possibly enter any orifice of our bodies. For we had been immunized.

Sweaty, grimy, tired and oh so terribly hungry, we settled in for an unusually long four-hour pause at the tremendously tacky Ramses Hilton pea-colored leatherette covered lounge bar. The *Ramses Hilton's* sister hotel is the *Hanoi Hilton*! We decided to just relax and have some liquid refreshments after checking in, following the conclusion of the second-leg of this around-the-world scavenger hunt/race. We didn't even bother to check up on our race time standings or that of the other Human*Racers*. Figuring by now that the difficult to comprehend, fuzzy logic-advanced math formula scoring system that was used in the Asian leg, was clearly out of our league. We may have rolled the dice, but hapless fate, *Insh Allah* once again, would determine our not so divine providence. "We can only do what we can do!" we mumbled between many beers.

For the next 24 hours we also blew off any and all alternative extracurricular cultural activities in favor of some cold brew and salty pistachios. We had clearly had enough of ancient Egypt for one visit. No late night disco scenes where we could really rock the *casbah* were in our future. No day trips out of the city to a local oasis market area to experience the weekly camel auctions. No more shopping for dusty rugs, brass lamps or pseudo-antiques. The latter of which are, as a rule, prematurely aged by being pissed on and then buried for a week or two underground and then polished with sandpaper. No more cups of the tart but sweet, dried hibiscus tea amalgamation known locally as *karkadeh*. We weren't even remotely interested in answering the burning question of the day: Do the poor lonely shepherd boys read Stephen King, Jackie Collins or Robert Ludlum page-turners while tending to their flocks grazing in the green and black fields? Rumor has it that many of them actually read Salman Rushdie's novels wrapped in a cover of the infamous "*Protocols of the Learned Elders of Zion!*" But that was wholly unsubstantiated! No, we were hereby determined to establish a new Muslim country world's record bar bill. We weren't moving from this genetic cocktail bar.

Like receiving a bad set of directions or having a particularly difficult clue to solve, the Human*Race* press corps also became yet another obstacle in the race to overcome. And as our madcap global scavenger hunt progressed, the international press was becoming more and more difficult to deal with. Kind of like having fleas. They had collectively started to ask some really tough and probing questions that were becoming increasingly harder to address. Seeking, what I suppose they thought was a short-cut to our souls. Such as: Why are you doing this? "For the adventure of course!" we would inevitably answer. Or my oft used, glib personal favorite: "Because it's there!" Then there was: What do you hope to gain by all this? Answer: "Nothing less than fame and fortune!" What has been your best experience so far? Quickly Andy would retort, "Airline food!" Do you miss your jobs and families back home? "What jobs and family back home?" we would both chorus.

What have you enjoyed the most while visiting Egypt? "Sleep!" was our usual reply. How can you justify such an extravagant holiday? Here's when we usually got a little defensive: "Holiday? Are you nuts? This is work pal." And the toughest prying question of them all: Who are you? Blank stares all around. "No comment." Real stumpers to be sure, even for the most philosophically jaded of tourists.

Prior to our hunkering down in the diarrhea green vinyl-covered lounge bar, we had granted an interview to a *Los Angeles Times/Associated Press* human interest writer, nay, now roving foreign correspondent, in the relative safety of our own luxury command, control and communications HQ center/hotel suite. Up to this point we had kind of played hard-to-get with the international media hounding the racers at every destination. We were hoping to build up our enigmatic personalities. As a result, we noticed that the folks bringing up the back of the Human*Race* pack were getting all the best human interest ink. Color pictures, pithy quotes, the whole fifteen minutes of fame bit. It was now our turn to jump center stage. Besides, we both figured, this was for a major paper back home in America. We had been selective in the hope that people we knew might actually read about us versus getting an essentially meaningless cover story, in, say, the *Indonesian Observer*, the *South China Morning Post* or the evening edition of the *Egyptian Gazette*. This was for a real hard-news syndicated columnist.

But then again, I'm too selective Andy would tell me, "You can tell that you're not in show bizness…you know, there's no such thing as bad ink!" he says. "Besides, you never know when you'll be a tax exile somewhere in Indonesia or other South East Asian backwater and a cover story might come in handy when you're putting together your next scam…uh…I mean business venture." Good point, I thought!

The interview however proved to be an all too typical Q & A session, and quite frankly, we both grew bored quickly. Like hormone producing teenagers sitting in a boring geometry class, our attention spans had been reduced to a nanosecond. But, we had to focus on the immediate task at hand. It was vitally necessary for us to put the proper spin on our already hazy bio's and add our enlightened thoughts at large about the race for the upcoming feature article.

Fortunately Andy and I had become unwitting experts at media manipulation during the 80's. We were masters at perception management. Media trained and ready for action. Hell, for eight seemingly endless years we cynically learned all there was to know about the many insidious forms of press management from those felonious thugs in the Reagan Administration. In fact, we, like so many other gullible Americans, spent the formative years of our lives watching the infamous Great Communicator spin his cartoonish web of lies to the star-struck American electorate. A type of media dictatorship had taken over America for the better part of the decadent decade. As if through osmosis, we learned all about the six-second sound-bite mentality, the correct angles for shooting back-drop photo-ops, spin-control, doublespeak, the many uses of strategic disinformation leaks, and the now famous message-of-the-day, from the Pied Piper of the TV screen himself. We witnessed Reagan's PR goons tame the entire news media from that of an ever vigilant watchdog during the Watergate era of the mid 1970's, to nothing more than a mindless mouthpiece for his corrupt Administration by the end of the Go-Go, Greed is Good 1980's. And none of which was technically lost on us.

Nonetheless, we've learned to be, oh just a tad, skeptical as to the press' accuracy in its passive reporting of events and in its mainstream analysis of current geopolitical events. It used to be that all that really mattered to us was getting them to spell our names correctly: that's Bill Chalmers, C-H-A-L-M-E-R-S, and Andy Valvur, V-A-L-V-U-R! But now it's equally as important to plant the seeds of questions in the mind of the writer of the story and eventually the reader. We were modern day practitioners of Roger Ailes-like spin control. Madison Avenue look out!

So, as we politely and ever so thoughtfully responded to some incredibly inane questions, we amused ourselves by watching a surrealistic event taking place from our hotel room balcony. As the reporter jotted down notes and quotes into a dog-eared steno-pad, we both looked in disbelief out the window. Amidst the continuous onslaught of blaring automobile horns coming from downtown Cairo and the yellowy-dust filled pale urban skyline, we watched a heroic lone water-skier slaloming up, or was it down?, the River Nile. He weaved gracefully from side to side with great precision. Carefully dodging, no doubt, the odd floating water buffalo carcass or two, as he carefully tried to remain upright. A fall into the sewer-brown polluted waters might have resulted in the skier contracting a potentially fatal dose of river blindness. Or worse! As we watched this perilous feat in utter amazement, we served up some incredibly bite sized, easy-to-remember, fun-to-read-about, sure-to-stick, wholly glib and surely superficial quotes about our great adventure traveling around the world. Words of wisdom from the great white travelers from America became the theme. Or so we thought. The version that ultimately appeared in a popular American magazine (No names please!) turned out to be a stinging attack on the Human*Race* in general, and on JB's personality in particular. But the writer liked us. I guess our spin control worked!

Sitting at the bar, drinking our acidic tasting *Camel Lager* brewed in of all places the Kingdom of Jordan, we took to reading week old newspapers and doing postcards. We tried hard to avoid the idle bar chit-chat with the ever present Egyptian lounge lizards, by pretending to speak only rare dialects of Canadian Eskimo and pre-Soviet Estonian. It seemed to work. No one sat near us and the unobtrusively polite bartender just refilled our glasses whenever they were a sip or two away from becoming empty. Apparently nobody noticed that we were reading English newspapers. Maybe nobody cared? The papers were filled with direly ominous signs from the European Continent. A potential French rail strike awaited us and untimely thirty-six degree weather in Paris were not the least bit encouraging. Although the news from Europe was bad, we didn't really mind because at this point we had a decent *Eurobuzz* going. A Eurobuzz is that giddy feeling of an imminent landing on the continent. It isn't unusual for people on the verge of a European vacation to fall victim to this malaise about two or three days before they depart. We also couldn't help but notice that Egyptian President Hosni Mubarak seems to have an incredibly hectic schedule and that he had his picture in the *Egyptian Gazette* no less than twelve times. Now that's a good press agent. "Ed Meese's evil twin, Michael Deaver finally got another job!" I suggested to Andy. "Maybe a new world record?" Andy retorted. We'd have to check, but we think ex-New York City Mayor Ed Koch holds the unofficial record of fourteen in an edition of the scandalous *New York Post*. This, we thought, was taking the cult of personality trip a bit too far. Moby, as we took to calling him, was posed with members of the Egyptian soccer team, two visiting foreign trade delegations, a fact finding World Bank rep, a hundred year old local Muslim cleric, with his wife at a state dinner for a visiting head of state from Mali, a State Department official for lunch, the always touring Mother Theresa, several senior members of the PLO, an anxious looking Israeli businessman, a little girl from Alexandria who won a science fair, or was it a spelling bee? And finally, a friendly pose with world famous actor Charlton Heston. The latter was no doubt here attempting another crossing of the Red Sea! Old actors don't fade away, they just go into politics.

We were getting pretty silly, (read: shit faced!) by the time duty called once again. The *GEO Magazine* group, consisting of a road weary French writer, named Maurice, and his young energetic American photographer, Debra, covering the entire 40,000 miles of the race, summoned all the HumanRacers together for a special group photo. It was to be shot in front of the crumbling lion-faced Sphinx and the three famous *Pyramids of Giza*. Unfortunately it was to be a sundown photo-op which of course meant that we had to venture out of our now comfortable home-away-from-home bar and face the harsh realities of chaotic Cairo at the height of rush hour.

Five o'clock traffic here makes the San Diego freeway look tame by comparison. There are only two traffic rules here: 1) Honk your horn continuously; and 2) Whoever gets to point 'A' first has the right-of-way. Forget about common courtesy. Stop signs and red lights are but mere suggestions here. Watch out for the hordes of jaywalking pedestrians and assorted desert livestock crossing the pot-hole filled road in front of you. The well-known California stop, a rolling non-stop, quickly followed by right-on-red turns are always possible, but rarely safe. The sidewalks are sometimes better known as the Egyptian equivalent of car-pool lanes. It's total unadulterated madness. Vehicular anarchy. Tempers flare, horns toot in stereo and nervous tourists are left to white knuckle it out in the backseats of beat up old taxicabs. All while Abdul plays Richard Petty on a dusty downtown Cairo side street. Determined lawlessness rules the road. Glad we opted for the optional collision-damage wavier offer.

It's not surprising at all to note that a recent *Nile TV News/Cairo Dispatch* poll shows that six out of ten Cairenes take tranquilizers once they are safe at home and out of the traffic in what is surely the world's noisiest city. After reading this tidbit, I lectured Andy to the effect that I had officially recognized that mankind as a species, had failed miserably. Because it hit me that for the first time in history, the wilderness was safer than civilization, but then again, after four long hours holed up in the hotel's bar I could say anything. At least we were fully fortified and prepared for the twenty mile journey to the pyramids.

Immense, mysterious, almost menacing, the sun-drenched golden pyramids of Giza, located southwest of Cairo, loomed over the horizon. Anticipation grew as we got closer to this celebrated ancient necropolis. We were told, over and over again, by amateur Egyptologists, that the three great Pyramids: Khufu (*Cheops*), Khafre (*Chephren*) and Menkaure (*Mycerinus*), were all that was left, the only modern day survivors of the much talked about Seven Wonders of the Ancient World. (*Quick, name the other six!?*) Proud monuments of a civilization that took the art of dying to grandiose epic proportions. The Giza monuments are among the oldest surviving man-made structures in the world. Each of the millions of finely-cut limestone blocks used to assemble these ancient tombs weigh about two-and-a-half tons each. It takes a lot of unskilled day laborers working without cranes and power tools, a long time to come up with enough blocks to bury a Pharaoh. *Cheops*, the Great Pyramid, was built around 2,800 BCE, and is the largest of the three topping out at just under five-hundred feet. Its gargantuan mass comprises over two million blocks. The sheer size of the Pyramids which house the tombs of the so-called nobles, is impressive enough, but to further comprehend that it took thousands of non-union slave masons years to build them five thousand years ago, adds to the immensity of this community special arts project.

Wonders of the Ancient World
Cheops Pyramids of Giza, Egypt
Hanging Gardens of Babylon, Iraq
Statue of Zeus (Olympia), Greece
Temple of Artemis (Diana) at Ephesus, Turkey
Tomb of King Mauslos/Mausoleum at Halicarnasus,
Colossus at Rhodes, Greece
Pharos (Lighthouse) of Alexandria, Egypt

While a tribal photo of the entire Human*Race* cast was taken, we watched in amusement as three young Arab vandals tried to fix the five thousand year old ruins by putting century old fallen pieces of stone back in place. "This couldn't be good for the tourist industry," I muttered to Andy. "They do things a little differently here!" he grinned.

A *cause celebre* of sorts had taken place a few days earlier. And despite our coincidental arrival on the same day, we categorically deny any involvement whatsoever with the event. Apparently a seven-hundred pound chunk of the Sphinx's shoulder had fallen off. It seems that in broad daylight and in full view of hundreds of tourists and locals alike, a giant portion of the forty-six century old Father of Terror unceremoniously crumbled off. This half-man, half-lion hybrid lying 840 feet long in the hot desert heat, built by Khafre, the son of Pharaoh Khufu as an offering to the ancient sun god Ra, had finally proved mortal. Or maybe not! At any rate, it apparently had the local *Egyptian Antiquities Organization* (EAO) officials in a tizzy as to how and why such a thing could have happened. It was a true embarrassment.

It is known locally as "The Riddle of the Sphinx." Several competing theories were put forth: New Age saboteurs disgruntled over the lack of press coverage their *Harmonic Convergence Day* received, had dynamited the old lion; the restoration specialists had screwed up royally and cleaned the glue-like mortar a little too well; many speculated that the stone fell due to natural erosion caused by unnatural air pollution and/or the rising hyper-saline Nile River; and finally, greed was a potential motive (antiquities theft) nasty art dealers could sell off the tiny pieces on Fifth Avenue. How somebody could haul off and sell broken unidentifiable pieces of rock was beyond my limited archeological grasp. And who in their right mind would actually buy them!? But then again, they've been selling pieces of the alleged Berlin Wall on the streets of New York City recently!

The cultural disaster had created an incredible local uproar. "No need to feel embarrassed," I reassured anybody who would listen. "The contracting job was done long before the new regime had come to power, and hence, they could always blame it on some other regime's mismanagement." To think that this enduring and mysterious edifice had survived thousands of years of inhospitable desert weather conditions, a continuous onslaught of foreign armies, and hordes of tourists and then out of the blue a piece falls off. Well, shit happens! Or, as our philosophical camel-caravan leader simply replied over and over again, "*Insh-Allah.*" It began to have a certain fatalistic ring to it, I thought.

We had had enough of Egypt; enough of its dusty, hot climate and its ancient history. We'd grown weary of personally handing out foreign aid to most of Egypt's exploding population base. We had had enough of slippery fast-talking antiquities peddlers, expert guides, black-veiled women, and seen way too many marbled mosques and towering minarets. We had had enough of bumpy camel rides around the Great Pyramids, dusty donkey rides in Luxor and hair-raising taxicab rides through the clogged Cairo streets. We had had enough of traffic delays, inefficiency delays and five times-a-day prayer delays where pious Arabs would bump their foreheads to the dirty pavement. We had had enough of it all. They say, whoever in hell *they* are, that you never really know a place until you're bored there. Maybe so, but we weren't gonna stick around long enough to find out.

As quickly as the photo session was over we returned to the relative safety of our hotel. Tomorrow morning we would be heading for Paris. Ah Paris. I could hardly wait. Andy was already reciting the names of savory foods he planned on devouring. But tonight we had to play the visiting celebrity game once again for the local media. We were invited to attend a lavish banquet/reception to be held in our honor at the grandiose *Nile Hilton Belvedere Nightclub.*

We gathered for several cocktails of unchilled vodka with the usual suspects at around 7 p.m.. At the reception we were greeted by a particularly nasty local pack of wolves, known collectively as the evening news. Several members of the group who were now suffering from the much dreaded *Pharaoh's Revenge* weren't able to attend the dinner party. They were immediately put on the HumanRace disabled list. By now, Andy and I had the celebrity routine down cold. However, we were reluctant participants in the game.

Over the years, Andy and I had learned to be gracious and civil in our own uncivil ways. From tattered jeans to pressed tuxedos, from outdoor beer bash barbecues to champagne and caviar receptions, we were comfortably at ease with ourselves. *Anyplace, anytime* is our proud motto.

After all, we had gone to the International School of Diplomacy and graduated *magna cum laude*. We were cool and elusive players, answering the most difficult of questions in mono-syllabic words. *Tip*: Always keep some food in your mouth so your speech is garbled and drink quickly so that you have an excuse to take your leave for another round at the bar. *Tip*: Of course, there's always the universally acceptable "I've got such a small bladder" appeal. We elusively avoided the group Q & A interview sessions. We shmoozed very little and quickly posed for the now dreaded obligatory Human*Race* group photos. A few weeks after the race I noticed in the photos that everybody always had the same clothes on! To be sure, it was yet another test of our now refined diplomatic skills.

"Please pass the sweet and sour sauce," I would politely ask. "Yes sir, Cairo is a wonderful world-class city replete with a grand history, beautiful architecture, charming people and a rich ancient culture." Andy would confidently reply, "No ma'am, we don't take positions on political issues such as the complex Arab-Israeli situation. We are traveling goodwill ambassadors for all people." We would both indulge in a lot of finessing. Valvur claims that the routine is pretty much like doing a tight fifteen minutes of stand up comedy in places like Branson or Truckee, where the press is relegated the part of the obnoxious heckler. Easy for him to say. At least he gets paid for his services.

We half-heartedly ate a dinner consisting of a yellowish wilted salad of questionable organic origin. I dared not attempt having any of the "Soap [sic] of the Day!" This was followed by some type of appetizer that smelled like that terrible smell you encounter in a subway bathroom. To help in the digestion of the meal, a sulfurous tasting bottle of red wine that surely came from grapes grown along the salty waters of the Red Sea was served. And finally, the main course. It was unidentifiable and remains a mystery to this very day. "Was it lamb, beef or veal?" were the most often asked questions raised by our dinner party. "Did it have two wings or four legs? Maybe it swam?" queried Andy. "Who really knows..." I replied. "Look at our host's faces. Even they don't know." We were sending out a culinary *SOS*. I wondered for a moment if I hadn't inadvertently eaten anything on some endangered species list!

Finally the racing results for Round Two were revealed by the Human*Race* organizers. JB, and his trusted entourage of mathematicians, secretaries, systems analysts, tourist torturers, accountants and PR men, had been up to their old tricks once again.

It was a cloudy situation. Andy and I just kind of stared at each other. Although we actually lost ground to the leaders of this certifiable crazy persons race, we had somehow managed to move up two full notches in the standings. Go figure? We now placed a respectable third out of the fifteen remaining teams, just a few hours off the leaders pace. "Buts!" "What ifs?" and "How could they..." buzzed through many of the assembled racing teams. Once again, not everyone was delighted with the results. It was a *yin-yang* situation for us, that we didn't fully understand, but nonetheless accepted as our fate. *Insh Allah!* We could still win this global debacle and become famous world travelers and do those *American Express* "You don't know us, but..." commercials. But how?

Deafened by the call of the muezzins, who were intent on not letting us sleep, severely overdosed on caffeine and still unable to shake off our severe jet-lag and reset our temperamental biological clocks, we called it a day. One last Arabic night awaited us. And instead of continuing this pointless socializing, we opted for temporary paralysis and hoped for sweet dreams of Paris. One last chance to have the hotel's staff impress us. We ordered room service. An hour later they brought us a couple of warm beers and a prayer rug. "Could this be our magic carpet ride out?" I rhetorically asked Andy.

Missing...But Presumed To Be Having A Good Time?

Another *o-dark-thirty* wake up call. 3:47 a.m. to be exact. Yet it seemed entirely worth the minor inconvenience of being rousted from our warm beds, because a few short hours away lay French cuisine. Besides, we weren't really sleeping, just enduring another night of tossing about, while suffering from our now extremely chronic cases of jet lag induced insomnia. We were leaving the chaos of Egypt and were very happy about our European prospects. We were headed for the Culinary Promised Land...Paris.

In Arabic they have dozens of apt sayings that you cannot escape hearing over and over again. One in particular, *Haraka, baraka!*, loosely translated meaning "motion is a blessing." We were about to be blessed. Been there. Done that. Don't want to go back. A *TWA* Tristar L-1011 en route to Paris turned out to be our much welcomed juggernaut out of the Third World. Our fondness for airline food grew by the minute as we anticipated our Western inflight meal. But even better, we were headed for a country that invented cholesterol. *Vive la France! Vive la difference!* From ancient civilization to a modern day society. A mere two thousand miles away, but two thousand light-years ahead in time. Not bad for a four hour flight. Our inter-hemispheric traveling spree was about to begin anew.

Security at Cairo International wasn't as tight as you'd like to think. No torturous body-cavity searches. Although Andy mentioned that at this particular juncture of the three-week old trip, he personally would have considered it a sensual act of safe sex to be frisked by strong female Norwegian border guards! No comment came from me.

You'd think that this being the Middle-East, that there would be a few thermal neutron analysis bomb detectors kicking around the airport's security checkpoints, or a few high-tech computer-enhanced gamma-ray machines. Nope. Just the usual metal detecting x-ray devices. Our now large and bulky carry-on bags weren't hand-searched and those cute bomb sniffing canines weren't in evidence in the terminal area. There were no patrolling battalions of armed military guards. Minimal security indeed. Given how efficiently the rest of the country was run we half expected to hear, after take off, an accented voice announce over the PA, "Ladies and gentlemen. American Imperialists and Zionist murderers. We are commandeering this capitalist corporate property to Lebanon." Nevertheless, I paid particularly close and careful attention to our jet's flight path that first half hour as we began crossing over the peaceful blue Mediterranean Sea. I for one, was ready to eat my American passport for an early breakfast snack if necessary and was nervously brushing up on my romantic Icelandic phrases; the only phrases I knew. Andy was on his knees in the aisle praying to *Joseph of Cupertino*, the Patron Saint of Airline Travelers! Nonetheless, no sweeping right turn East took place. We were temporarily out of harm's way and heading north-by-northwest on a trans-Mediterranean course. There would be no hostage taking today. "We must be up-to-date with our petro-dollar interest payments to the desert emirs," I noted to Andy. But then again, as wise men say, we're all hostages to airplane discomfort once the plane is off the tarmac.

We arrived at *Aeroporte Roissy-Charles de Gaulle* International in *gay Paree* around 1 p.m. for the home stretch sprint across the European Continent. The Human*Race's* endgame was nearing. And we were prepared for a tough fight. We were lean and mean by this point in the race. Battle hardened and traveler check ready. We were very relieved to have had the foresight to have continually shipped boxes home along the way as we inevitably acquired more and more tourist trophies. Most of the stuff had been required scavenges, like: incense sticks, Chinese calligraphy, wood carvings, brass ear spoons, traditional Arab garb and the like. While some of the other stuff included the more functional peace offerings for our respective mates back home. We were carrying those items.

Now I'm not gonna start offering you any cheap, though well advised, travel advice, like so many of those uptight specialty travel magazines. Far be it from me to offer the discerning reader and/or travel enthusiast, a potpourri of wholly subjective and equally unsolicited time-dated travel tips. I just tell it like it is. No hotel reviews. Okay, not too many anyway! No pompous restaurant recommendations. Well, bad food is bad food. Certainly no cruise ship line or car rental agency comparisons. No pointers on tipping, or bribing, or on Third World best-buy bargain hunting. No travel advisories and certainly no unsolicited destination ideas. That's just not me. No way.

But, on the other hand! A savvy travel junkie always remembers ten basic traveling commandments:

Commandment No. 1: You need money. Without proper funding, you ain't going anywhere. Now, of course, this varies in magnitude. Obviously your monetary needs are significantly different in Geneva, Switzerland than in, say, Ensenada, Mexico. And it clearly costs more to bribe a nasty AK-47 machine gun-toting Russian Border Guard than a friendly look-the-other-way Thai hotel manager. Nonetheless, adequate funds are required. So always have some type of positive equity position available at your immediate disposal, such as: gold bullion, *VISA, Mastercard, American Express*, a well-financed trust fund to dip into, extremely liquid muni-bonds, marketable real estate, diamond jewelry, travelers checks of any make or denomination, rich friends or support-ive relatives, or just cold hard cash. Vacant land will do nicely in a pinch. American twenties seem to be the international monetary unit of choice. In the developing world, keep a healthy supply of ones on hand too. They're great for incidental tipping and a handful are great when you need to employ the local youth for diversionary purposes.

Commandment No. 2: Always return home with gifts. It is vitally important in assuring your domestic bliss, no matter what your marital status. Repeat, always return from a trip with trinkets and baubles. The more the better. No matter how big or how small. Gold, silver and large loose precious stones are the big winners by far. Handcrafted earrings and leather products always go over well, as do exotic clothes and serious art pieces. Black velvet paintings of Madonna, Elvis or Charles Bronson, and anything with the destination's name stamped on it, just won't do at all. T-shirts aren't happening either. Trust me on this one!

Commandment No. 3: If you can't carry it, don't take it! Sounds simple enough, but there's a few qualifiers to this one. By carrying, I do mean carrying onto the plane, not checking-in at the curb with a friendly sky-cap. To successfully insure your international traveling bliss never, repeat never, check baggage. The only deviation from this cardinal rule is, if you're on your last leg home with gifts in tow *(See Commandment No. 2)* and can't carry it all on board the plane, check your dirty laundry, not the peace offerings/gifts. It's better to have lost dirty laundry than arriving home with laundry, but *sans* presents.

This last basic travel truth became more and more self-evident as our race around-the-world raged on. On several occasions we heard horror stories by fellow Human*Race* contestants of baggage delays and actual lost luggage. We simply would not let something like this happen to us. We're practicing existentialists and destiny is clearly in our own hands. So we followed our third travel commandment in both spirit and to the letter.

It is an extreme hassle to first check-in your luggage, and then have to wait, sometimes for days, at the revolving carousel to pick up your bags at the other end. But god forbid you should lose anything. A lot of travelers don't realize that under the antiquated 1917 *Warsaw Convention Agreement* (Yes, *1917* it's no typo!) when they were still flying tri-planes so weight and space was clearly at a premium, you can only receive a mere $9.07 per pound ($20 per kilo) in compensation for your lost, stolen, and/or misplaced possessions with a weight cut-off maximum of seventy pounds per bag. That's only $634.90 total! Shit, a pair of those aerodynamically-designed *Air Nikes*, previously owned stone-washed *501 Levi's* and your basic casual *Armani* sports jacket cost more than that. And that's not even counting the cost of the designer leather luggage itself! Hell, under the same so-called *Agreement*, (I never agreed to this shameful act!) airlines are only obligated to pay just $75,000 per wrongful death airline crash victim. My unsolicited advice is to find a good litigation attorney for better results. Remember, reasonable doubt at reasonable prices. Needless to say, follow these simple tips from the Valvur & Chalmers School of Global Grazing and don't ever check baggage.

10 Commandments of Travel
Always be adequately liquid and have enough cash.
If you don't return home with gifts, don't come home.
If you can't carry it, don't take it!
It's better to call ahead for a cab then trying to wave one down on the street.
Pay with credit cards whenever possible, better exchange rates and buyer protection.
Reconfirm everything!
Negotiate for everything!
Take the first flight out of the day to your next destination, leaving room for error.
Always see your room before you take it.
Tip BIG when you arrive, everyone will know you and treat you like royalty!

Our global trans-cultural crime spree reached zenith proportions in of all places, spectacularly beautiful and always romantic Paris. Of all our exotic, tropical and historical Human*Race* destinations, that thus far had included: Hong Kong, Malaysia, Java, Bali and the many desert towns we visited along the River Nile, it upset us all the more that one of our personal favorite world-class cities would witness our brand of cultural terrorism first hand. And we would be the culprits. We begged the vacation gods to show us a little mercy. We hoped that no one we knew saw us committing any unnatural cultural acts in Paris.

We were like kids in the proverbial candy store, with expense accounts to boot. The only thing we lacked, and were distressingly growing ever so short of at this point, was time itself. What an elusive commodity. And unfortunately for us, most of our few short hours in Paris were to be spent wide-eyed and wanting; our noses pressed eagerly against the window of our taxi. We anguished over our plight in heaven-on-earth as we watched a plethora of corner *cafe-tabacs* (There are over 12,000 cafes in Paris!), haughty *Rive Gauche* galleries, alluring Parisian women, glorious architecture, old men wearing *berets*, *Metro* stations, countless bakeries, theaters, bustling wide boulevards, famous museums and churches, engaging street performers, green parks, more lanky Parisian legs, and numerous bistros and fine restaurants whisk past us at blinding speeds. Our eyes welled up with tears on more than one occasion. Of all weekends to be in a hurry too. It was that once-a-year special weekend celebrating the uncorking of the famous *Beaujolais-Nouveau* for 1989 harvest year. The horror, the horror, bless me Father for I have sinned.

Sightseeing *per se*, is a tad redundant in Paris. The entire town, aptly called the City of Light, is a sight to behold in and of itself. This modern day capital of contemporary Western Civilization, with Egypt currently in image rehab, and home to nine million urbane Parisians, beckoned us to come play with it for a while. At least for a quick refreshing weekend we thought. You know, tour the side alleys of *Rue de Lappe* and *Montparnasse*, or *St. Germain des Pres* in the Latin Quarter, mingle merrily in the late night jazz bars, dine at one of the countless exquisite restaurants that line

Rue LaFayette, or maybe even have a French-style picnic with brie, wine and a baguette, among the hallowed tombstones of such cultural-icons as: Moliere, Chopin, Proust, Oscar Wilde, Sarah Bernhardt and Jim Morrison, in the 100-acre *Pere Lachaise Cemetery*. Is this too much to ask? We are grown ups and surely we deserved a weekend pass from life. After all, we had just emerged from four frustrating days and nights in what seemed like the cultural trash heap of history. We wanted real culture. Some real food. Some real wine. Some real female company. But alas, poor us, it was not to be, for we would be leaving Paris all too quickly. Before sundown if all went according to plan!

Before undertaking any of our assigned tasks in Paris, we were going to fully enjoy one simple meal that we had been dreaming about for days in tasteless Cairo. In fact, at one point in our Middle Eastern journey, we had even fantasized about being greeted by a huffy ill-mannered *maitre d'* and getting served by an equally rude table *garcon*.

After enjoying a wonderfully tasty steak and *frites* lunch, washed down with a delicious fruity bottle of *rouge*, capped off with a steaming sweet cup of *cafe au lait*, we reluctantly resigned ourselves to our fate. Paris was now ours, but only for a very short three hours.

To add insult to the emotional wounds we were now licking, the thoughtless, mean spirited, uncultured, nasty, pagan worshipping Human*Race* organizers, JB in particular, had given us equally unpleasant tasks to perform in Paris. Theirs was an all too typical touristy, and wholly unchallenging list of scavenges to perform. Up to now, all the tasks had been either remotely interesting or at least culturally challenging. But this time JB had lapsed. The Paris scavenge list included all those must see spots that you'd visit during a week's stay here. We, of course, would visit them all in three short hours, queues and all.

No creativity was spared us during this belittling pseudo-cultural exercise. After the experiences of the Asian leg and all that we had seen there, we expected to visit *Les Egouts* (the sewers) or even the stuffy catacombs lodged beneath Paris's grand boulevards. Those would have made for some wild photo-ops. Or perhaps we would be required to obtain a ticket stub from the famous neoclassical Opera House, or even more challenging, from the recently completed ultra-modern *Opera de la Bastille*. Perhaps a short shopping spree at the famous *Marche aux Puces* (Flea Market). Here we could have browsed through 3,000 stands and stalls searching for traditional flea market bric-a-brac. Any of which would have been truly cultural achievements. Better yet, a quick trip out to Louis the XIV's stately mansion of *Versailles* or an enchanting evening boat ride down the dramatically lit *River Seine*. As it was, we were stuck with the beautiful but mundane. Nothing we hadn't already done a half a dozen times before.

First we spent eight hectic minutes at the world famous and newly expanded *Louvre* in pursuit of the even more famous painting by Leonardo da Vinci, the "*Mona Lisa*." Billed as the "world's largest museum" with over 3,000 masters spread out over 400,000 square feet of exhibition space, one usually requires at least an hour or two, or three...to view the so called significant works alone. Eight whole minutes. We spent more time debating Monsieur I.M. Pei's controversial ultra-modern glass and steel pyramid entrance (We both approved of it's architectural integrity.) than we did visiting with the likes of the timeless and sexy 2nd Century BC "*Venus de Milo*" statue or catching a fast glimpse at Jacques-Louis David's "*Coronation of Napoleon*." A cultural crime of epic proportions that we truly detested committing.

Then it was up the grandest of all the Grande boulevards in the proud Republic of France, the cafe and boutique lined-*Champs-Elysee* for a quick photo op at the *Arch de Triomphe*. Then on to the *Eiffel Tower*, one of the Seven Wonders of the Modern World (*Quick, name the other six!?*), which happened to be celebrating its 100th Anniversary, for a quick aerial view of cloudy central Paris. I literally had to pull Andy away from this scenic attraction, for he had fallen in love again with his mind's eye equivalent of Bernardo Bertolucci's famed Juliet. A tall brunette he met at the Eiffel Tower. Too bad he didn't get her phone number. He was tired!! I don't think he would have ever made a mistake like that at home.

I had to drag him away for from the anniversary party for an even hastier photo-op with the Gothic and romantic *Notre-Dame* cathedral, an ice cream cone from the world renowned *Berthillon Cafe* located on the sedate cobble-stoned streets of *Ile St. Louis*, and we were done! Just that simple. As quickly as I have just reflected and wrote about our tasks, we had completed all the scavenges. Not very creative, eh? Bottom line: we kicked some ass in Paris.

Wonders of the Modern World
Crystal Palace, England
Eiffel Tower, France
Empire State Building, USA
Golden Gate Bridge, USA
Louisiana Superdome, USA
Panama Canal, Panama
North Sea Protection Works, Netherlands

Our polite and extremely curious taxi driver whisked us across *Pont-Neuf* then quickly by the *Centre Georges Pompidou's Les Halles* neighborhood. From the back seat of our non-stop dash to *Gare du Lyon* we dreamed of the pleasant sights of Paris that we were missing, like: Napoleon's *Pantheon*, the famous *Ritz*, the fabulous museums of Picasso, *La Villette, Beaubourg, d'Orsay*, and off in the distance, the white cathedral of *Sacre-Coeur*. What a shame it was. With Paris' sophisticated cafe culture quickly fading into the foggy cool evening, we headed ever so reluctantly to the train station. We weren't happy campers.

We arrived at *Gare du Lyon* station with just enough time to perform our ritual dance, the *train schedule boogaloo*. We were at a difficult juncture in the race where the slightest timing error could remove us from contention and the possibility of winning the whole Human*Race* *enchilada*. We had to formulate an extremely efficient plan for doing Europe. We hoped that it would prove better than Napoleon's or Hitler's strategies. We had to decide which path to travel: a due-east semi-circular route through slow and mountainous Switzerland and Austria; or take a southeastern, and seemingly more direct flat land approach. JB, the supreme commander of the Human*Race*, had given us a choice between two scavenges, along with which Continental Europe path to follow. We could leave Paris and go east to Strasbourg or southeast to Chambery. Either way we still faced an extensive list of scavenges in Milan, Verona, Venice and Ljubljana, Yugoslavia. Once we finished these tasks, we could fly home to New York-Kennedy from any *TWA* gateway. Our ticket was open.

Independently, Andy and I had each calculated what we thought would be the best, er, the quickest route possible. We compared notes, and found to neither of our surprise, that we mapped out the same travel itinerary. Thus our strategy was: Paris south to Chambery, east to Milan via Turin, onward east to Verona and Venice, and finally Ljubljana. Eventually, we'd head north into Austria and depart from Vienna on Monday at high-noon. We figured that all this train traveling and completing of all required scavenges, along with inevitable down time and friction we would encounter, would take us roughly sixty hours. *Europe in sixty hours!* We were poised on the brink of victory. Or so we thought.

As we quickly boarded the train and headed off into the night, we left several Human*Race* teams still pondering their respective travel plans at *Gare du Lyon* train station. Those crazy to understand ticket window lines can be rough. They were literally left in the train's vacuum, while we were in a cozy First Class compartment of the subsonic *Train Grande Vitesse* (TGV) bullet train headed south to Chambery. Having concurred with confidence on our route in advance and now speeding comfortably away at 186 mph, we figured we were in tall cotton. We're going for the gold. "We are big men!" we kept reminding ourselves over and over again as we raised our glasses in toast after toast. We sipped the grape from a choice wine list and sampled a selection of cheeses from our cushy seats. Our Chambery *ETA* was just three hours away. I took the time to make a few notes in my journal while Andy stared out the window muttering, "I'll never see her again. Never..."

The moon was full in the night sky when we arrived unannounced in sleepy little Chambery, located in close proximity to the French Alps at about 11 p.m. on a chilly Friday night. According to the train schedule, we had three hours to find our sole scavenge in this little French provincial town just miles from the Italian frontier. Time enough for a late night dinner, a few drinks and some tangoing at a local nightclub we thought! *Boy were we wrong.*

Between that ever present jetlag malaise that immobilizes you when you least expected it, and the race organizers flight of fancy errors in planning, we unfortunately used up all of our spare time in Chambery and didn't even have time for a quick little drink.

"*Chambery, France: Photograph both team members near the site of Leonardo da Vinci's tombstone.*" It seemed simple enough. This was our sole mission tonight. And although sporadic synapses of our memory data banks snapping back to a college art history class vaguely questioned the very nature of the task, we jogged out of the train station, our baggage in left luggage, full of boyish enthusiasm. Another adventure awaited us.

Armed with only a pen-sized mini-flashlight, we were about to become grave robbers of sorts. We secured a visitor's map of Chambery, no small achievement at nearly midnight in a small town of about fifty thousand, and asked for basic directions from the train station patrons (The *Office de Tourism* was of course closed.) and headed towards a cemetery located just outside the town's center. We figured that a man of the stature of the great Leonardo da Vinci at least warranted city center status. After climbing the cemetery's fence and spending well over thirty minutes groping around old and crumbling tombstones in the moon's shadowy glow, we decided that Leo wasn't there. Regrouping, we checked the tourist map once again and noticed a small, so-called Italian sovereign cemetery located up on the hill a few short kilometers away. Off we went with renewed passion. By now it seemed a lot colder than when we first left the train station and the mid-November frost was getting to us, along with the ridiculousness of our scavenge.

This time, we were in an even more secluded part of town and had to scale the ten-foot high stone wall of a medieval monastery guarding the enclosed grave yard. We were getting giddy at the thought of what we were doing, as we continued to search in vain for Leonardo's famed final resting spot. Trekking through a graveyard, even in your own neighborhood, is weird business in the best of times. Attacking one at the witching hour in a strange environment in a foreign country can be a little bit trickier. I'm not the least bit ashamed to admit that our skin crawled and neck hairs stood on end on more than a few occasions, as we shone our dimmer-by-the-minute flashlight across tombstone after tombstone. Still no luck. Andy, growing increasingly colder, had become very uneasy at this point; questioning the very philosophical nature of the HumanRace and our foolish parts in it. He required a stern talking to. We both decided to find somebody, anybody to ask specific, point it out on our map, questions. Enough of this midnight wandering.

By now it was closing time for a few of the village's downtown bars. We backtracked to the city center and accosted numerous startled couples romantically strolling home from an evening of drinking and dancing. Needless to say, many of them were just a little too drunk to answer when they were served an odd mixture of text book French-Canadian with heavily punctuated English. It's funny how people look at you, kinda like puppies with their bent heads, when they can't quite comprehend your questions.

There we were, in a comical situation once again, in search of our Holy Grail: Valvur, in his New York City chic all black look, and yours truly playing Indiana Jones revisited, hat and all; asking poor drunk souls at midnight in the now freezing cold, "*Ou est la tombe de Leonardo da Vinci?*"

Well, to make a long story short. After getting some very strange looks, we were Americans in France least we forget, laughed at, sent deliberately in the wrong direction a couple of times and were totally ignored, we were no closer to finding Leo's sacred resting spot than when we left the train station hours ago. As Karl Malden always asks in those TV commercials: "*What do you do? What do you do?*" We decided to go to the nearest police station and ask directions!

As three local officers warily checked our dilated pupils for illegal substance abuse and our breaths for alcohol intoxication, we were skeptically allowed to stay in the Chambery police station lobby and ask a few probing questions. Let's see, it kind of went like this as I remember Andy explaining it to them: "This morning we were in Cairo, Egypt and flew into Paris where we spent three hours before boarding the TGV to arrive here in Chambery, where we're searching for Leonardo da Vinci's grave site. We're in a race around-the-world and plan to leave Chambery on the 2:30 a.m. train en route to Milan, Italy. We'll be back in New York on Monday." I ended his rather factual recollection of our recent events with a nod and an off-beat, "Yea, that's the ticket."

Steel jail cell doors never closed so fast as…No, no, we didn't get arrested or thrown into a padded cell. Although I'm quite sure they thought about it for a few moments in the silence that hung in the air after Andy's explanation. But, there are no laws against being idiots. And leaving Paris after only three short hours is certainly incriminating! Or for being a Yuppie American cultural terrorist, or for being total fools. At least not yet, anyway. The six policeman now eyeballing us in utter amazement all began to laugh at the same time. They laughed and laughed. They pointed at us and laughed out loud. They laughed so hard that tears began streaming down their faces. For the longest time they laughed. Valvur hadn't even been performing his killer comedy routine, but they laughed just the same at our expense. We had been reduced to a roving comedy team in the same vein as *Laurel and Hardy*. Or was it *Abbott and Costello*? It wasn't a pretty picture. But, it was laughable apparently.

Leonardo da Vinci's grave was nowhere near Chambery, we were summarily informed between bursts of gut-busting laughter. He wasn't even French they insisted, heckling us from behind their desks. Our mission was indeed a mission impossible. And so they laughed a hearty laugh until, totally dumbfounded, we looked at each other and started to laugh with them. As they say, if you can't beat em, join em. After a few slaps on the back and some sips of water to restrain the collective jocularity, we all became good friends. We had bonded. Laughter, the great equalizer once again.

In the end, they wrote us a note, "Our excuse from Chambery," we liked to call it. Documentation that we were indeed there in Chambery and Leonardo da Vinci wasn't. Dead or alive. A group photo of us together with all the policeman was taken and our one-night stand in Chambery was over. Eight by ten glossies would be sent out upon our return home. "*Merci beaucoup!*" was how we left them all smiling and waving us on. "*Bon voyage*," they told us. Out we went into the cold night air of Chambery. Laughter echoed down the street as we meandered back to the train station en route to Milan.

A postscript from Chambery: The ultra-talented Leonardo da Vinci died on the morning of the 2nd of May, 1519 in one of the King of France's many castles in *Cloux*, later named *Clos-Luce*, of apparent old age. And although he was buried nearby *Cloux*, in the village of *Amboise*, within the castle-chapel confines of St. Florentin's graveyard next to a group of other princes and nobles, his gravestone has since disappeared. Between the perils of violence encountered in war and revolution over 450 years, and the timeless greed of thieves, vandals and real estate developers alike, neither his remains nor his marker has ever been found. Or maybe not! At any rate, rest in peace Leo. The world is a richer place because you lived.

Italy is an interesting paradox. Despite their continuous changes of government over the years (As of this writing they've had fifty, you count 'em, different regimes since the end of World War II!) which according to my theories, carefully formulated from uncountable political science lectures, bouts of deconstructivist and historical analysis and extensive pain-staking documentation, clearly denotes a society in chaos. It is a political circus *maximus*. Yet upon closer examination, Italy functions. And functions very well I must add, despite their nation's on going game of musical chairs. Its vibrant commercial enter-prises, communications systems and transportation facilities, are all efficiently run. By the way, Italy ranks a distant second to the Banana Republic of Bolivia, which holds the *Guinness Book of World Records* of over 180 coups, counter coups and assorted revolutions in the past 164 years! I can only surmise that ever since their last dictator, the good olde boy Benito Mussolini, the skeptical Italians have preferred to do it themselves. That is, run their country without the longing or necessity of a strong father-like central government. But what do I know?

It was a dull and hazy overcast early morning when our train finally rolled into Milan at 8:30 a.m. The six hour ride from Chambery proved to be both physically exhausting and emotionally draining. I almost snapped in a fit of rage and considered throwing in the towel and heading for the Greek Isles, or maybe even the *Bulldog* cafe in Amsterdam! But Andy calmed me down by force feeding me a *Snickers* bar, which allowed me to continue the Human*Race*. It would have been such a waste of our last sixteen days on the road to have quit mid-stream, for the end was very near.

The *crisis du jour* this time was really not a crisis at all. Just an ill timed set of minor inconveniences that when I'm physically strong and intellectually alert, I usually overlook. But this time, I was just too tired mentally and physically weary to deal with them.

It kind of evolved like this. After leaving the Chambery Police HQ, we ventured back to the train station, cold and exhausted by our ordeal.

We had spent all of our leisure time because of JB's foul up. The train was due to arrive in less than an hour. No time for fun or frolic by then, all the bars were closed. Not that we could have, but its always good to keep your options open. Anyway, I ended up attempting to catch a quick forty winks in a steel luggage locker, while Andy was supposed to keep a watchful eye over me. Body snatchers you know. The station was now filled with homeless vagabonds, village drunks and your basic white on-the-go *Eurotrash*. The next thing I know, an extremely large saber toothed German Shepard police dog was growling menacingly at me as some jerk continually kicked my leg which was sticking out of the small cramped four foot long locker. Given a choice of how to be awakened from a blissful nap, this method would not be high on my list. So, I try to ignore them until I get kicked again and again, until I finally emerge from my humble sleeping chamber, only to glare at two of our police buddies from the local station making their nightly rounds. Guess what? They laughed once again, recognizing me and realizing that I was just harmlessly funny, as I rubbed my dry sandpaper-like contact lens filled eyes. "And so we meet again!" I gestured and smiled to them.

Andy then returned from a casual walk, *AWOL* from guard duty, just in time to catch the tail end of my unusual wake up call. "What was that all about?" he questioned me. "Nothing really," I told him a little pissed off. "But if we're ever in Alaskan grizzly bear country together, you're not pulling any guard duty," I growled.

Needless to say, this unpleasant episode set the tone for me for the next several hours. The train, as we saw it, was *SRO* out of Chambery en route to Milan. And at 2:30 in the morning that's not a very encouraging omen after an extremely long day that included an *o-dark-thirty* Cairo wake-up call, followed by a long flight to Paris and a bullet train ride to Chambery, followed by a frustrating wild-goose chase. I for one was dead on my feet and after surveying the entire length of the train, we happened upon a single empty and surely prized, First Class compartment. We lucked out once again I told Andy. I imagined that fate was being kind to us for all that we had endured that day. Time to catch some much needed *zzz's* I thought.

After settling in and marveling at our favorable situation we found out the real reason why the compartment had been empty. Unfortunately for us, the air conditioning unit was stuck in the high position. Not a healthy situation when you're in the freezing Italian Alps, tired, and coming down with something I would have clearly preferred to have left behind in Cairo. Overcoming certain frostbite, I bundled up enough to outwit this man-made environmental obstacle to attempt a *siesta*. Then the second reason why the compartment had been so conveniently empty introduced itself to us. A constant irritating clicking noise just about sent me off the deep end. *Click...click...click,* was all I could hear as I rubbed my hands together attempting to avert the cold. I menacingly eyeballed Andy as if I could kill. Oh, I knew it wasn't his fault, but we were slap happy. "Are we having fun yet?" I remember hearing him sarcastically ask. "Who's idea was this anyway?" I quickly parried. We became giddy. I then became extremely tense. And then all of a sudden, I snapped like a rubber band.

I wasn't a pretty sight as I ranted and raved, kicked and scratched, screamed and yelled. I questioned aloud the very soundness of our collective financial savvy in spending $15,000 for this special junket to hell. I was taking out all my three weeks worth of pent up road rage on the seats, ceiling, luggage racks and windows of our train compartment. *The Who* have been evicted from seedy Sunset Boulevard hotels for lesser atrocities. Thank goodness for that hidden *Snickers* bar that Andy seemed to have found just at the right moment. I calmed down instantly as I wolfed down the entire bar in a couple of bites. I growled. My rage slowly subsided. My blood pressure sunk. My fists unclenched. I released Andy from the headlock.

So with rejuvenated sugar-induced stamina, we finally made it into *Stazione Centrale* in downtown Milan. This time however, a lot worse for the wear. This adventure of a lifetime was stealing our lives away and I was getting sick. I could feel it coming. Like slow death. I envisioned the black plague. I could hear voices saying, "Bring out your dead. Bring out your dead." I was now an official member of the Human*Race's* walking, nay, make that the running wounded.

Milan, Italy's second city, is considered the business and financial center of the country and a beacon of fashion and design for the world. It is also the model capital of the world. We were told this by a usually reliable source employed in the downtown Los Angeles garment industry. He said, and I quote: "They actually grow models in Milan. Statuesquely tall, sturdy but gangly, stunningly stylish, pouty-lipped blonde high-fashion runway models." Given such profound strategic information, we sought to act upon it immediately on our arrival. So in addition to our required Human*Race* tasks, we added one unofficial scavenge of our own: "Locate a fashion model, attract her attention and get her to smile at our obvious wit and gentlemanly charm, and then get either her phone number or a picture." It was a self-imposed challenge of sorts. That's just the way we are. Two crazy guys running amok in Europe. We didn't want an old-fashioned Saturday night date or anything so time consuming. Just a name and a number or a photo and a smile. That would prove to be enough for us global voyeurs. It was a challenge, a dream, a wish, a hope, a desire, a fantasy, a yearning, a hunger, a blind ambition, and weird type of obscene craving to be sure. And since we had three hours to spend in Milan, it seemed worth the few minutes of effort for a latter day self-satisfying autoerotic fantasy. It was obvious, we had become totally delirious after sixteen long days on the road to nowhere.

A dense cloud of industrial toxins shrouded the city as we zipped past a tangerine-colored trolley in our lemon-yellow taxicab en route to our glass and chrome destination. Milan is that kind of town, stylish and color coordinated, but severely polluted. Our first stop was the impressive *Piazza del Duomo* and the equally famous 123-year-old massive iron-and-glass, cross-shaped Galleria food and shopping emporium extraordinaire. There we sipped some heavenly, though pricey, *espresso grandes* at a trendy outdoor cafe and watched this city of two million come alive. We had a thirty minute wait until the fairytale-like Gothic *Duomo* cathedral opened at 10. So we sat and watched the smart dressed Saturday morning Milanese shoppers and fully initiated our Model Watch program.

The giant *Duomo* dominates the Milanese skyline. Ground was broken in 1386 on what's reputed to be the "largest Gothic church in the world." We had become increasingly skeptical of any claims of being the largest, oldest, newest, tallest and one-and-only anything in the world during our trip. If the scaffolding out front is any indication, they're apparently still working on the *Duomo*. "Forever in progress," to paraphrase a taxi driver's broken English on the holy architectural project. After viewing all of its more than 3,000 hand-crafted statues, 135 spires, 96 gargoyles, dozens of stained glass biblical window scenes, hundreds of marble inscriptions, and single golden Madonnina on its roof, we were both glassy-eyed. We looked at each with vacant unconcerned stares. It was then that we realized we had officially succumbed to total *Monument Burnout.*

Sometimes called the *Stendhal Syndrome*, named after an 18th Century novelist turned tourist, *Monument Burnout* is a dreaded traveling disorder that inflicts itself on only the most jaded of globe-trotters. It causes occasional hallucinations, bouts of memory loss, severe disorientation and a particularly traumatic strain of *MEGO's.* Our rapid over-exposure during the last fortnight to so many of the world's great wats, stupas, temples and cathedrals, historic monuments, museums, grand palaces, religious shrines and amusement parks alike, had eroded our usually refined cultural sensibilities. Our brains had been reduced to mush. We had overdosed on culture and ethnic heritage. We were totally saturated and had become totally desensitized. We would have probably given a vintage "*Three Stooges*" episode a cold vacant stare. It was a case of too much art and too much history, in too many places, in too short a time. It was all down hill after this and we knew it. Although we would continue to physically visit many of Europe's glorious places, even taking their pictures with us in the foregrounds, we wouldn't actually be absorbing anything of substance after this impairing *apogee* of cultural overkill. We were two extremely over exposed puppies. Our frontal lobe cranium implanted software programs and artificial memory chips needed immediate purging.

But onward we went. Unofficially in search of models, officially however, our mission took us to the *Museo alla Scala*. We felt a relapse of *Monument Burnout* coming on again after a brief respite. If this had been Cleveland's Rock 'n' Roll Hall of Fame we might have been remotely interested. But our temperament being what it was by now, forget it. Opera!? Who are you trying to kid? Even in the best of times we're not that cultured.

The museum was built along side the world-famous *La Scala Opera House* where numerous operatic stars have made their professional singing debuts. We blew in and out of the museum in minutes. Amid a pack-rat collection of assorted opera memorabilia, we quickly located *bona fide* locks of Wolfgang Amadeus Mozart's hair, Wolfy to his friends, clay impressions of the renowned bandleader Toscanni's hands, and finally, a curious looking marble bust of the great tenor, Caruso. Bored to tears, we sought out another round of *espresso grandes* across town at the *Cafe della Grazie,* located just across the piazza from the stately confines of the Dominican monastery and *Basilica of Santa Maria della Grazie.* Still no model sightings yet. Although there had been a few false alarms.

You had to know that good old Leonardo da Vinci would weave his way into our gonzo travel adventure once again. First we met up with his *"Mona Lisa"* hanging in Paris' *Louvre Museum.* Next in Chambery with our now legendary midnight *"Raiders of the Lost Ark"* like search for his nonexistent crypt. And now here in Milan too. A type of recurring cultural nightmare we thought. On a dimly lit refectory wall inside the 15th Century walls of Santa Maria, Leo had struck again. This is Leonardo's historic and spiritually moving *"Last Supper."* This mega-famous fresco is in less than great shape however. Unfortunately, da Vinci's giant wall-sized mural has had a history of problems dating back to when he originally completed this papacy commissioned piece in 1495.

Now I'm just riffing here, playing back some idle bits and pieces I picked up from a college Art History class, but Leonardo, always the inventive type, used an untested oil-based pigment for his beloved fresco and it didn't set as well on the damp convent dinning hall wall as it should have. This, combined with centuries induced old age caused by the occasional insurance-scam fire, the odd B & E's, unsanctimonious looting, periodic flooding, natural decay, and a nasty barrage of carpet bombing by the Allied Forces during World War II, has rendered this majestic piece, oh just a tad, worse for wear. In a state of constant refurbishment, a crew of Japanese-funded restoration specialists are presently colorizing Leonardo's masterpiece in an attempt to preserve it for the ages. It probably looks better now than when he finished it some 500 years ago. The Ted Turner wannabe's of the art world to some. The saviors of Santa Maria's church-cum-tourist attraction cash register to others.

Things were getting grim. We were about to leave the fashion model capital of the Western World without ever having achieved a single actual model sighting. It was still too early in the morning we thought. We quickly passed by the brooding 15th-Century fortress of *Sfozza Castle*, located in the very heart of downtown Milan. Still nothing. We were blaming the problem on lack of vision caused by a foul smog that had wrapped itself around the city center. Our now battered egos had begun to conjure up numerous excuses. I figured that those shapely and leggy models were all still at home catching up on their beauty sleep. We decided our eyes were not the same after four days of ogling veiled Egyptian women and only three hours worth of recovery time in Paris. Totally dejected, we departed Milan and continued our journey, heading east towards Venice.

Our strategic objective all along was to arrive in Venice before night-fall. The reason being, that one of our Venetian scavenges was to pose with, *at least three*, of the zillions of disgusting, filthy and diseased piazza pigeons in famous San Marco square. In SoCal we refer to these polluted pesky pigeons as rats with wings. And that they are. Needless to say, we're no colombophile's, but being avid ornithologists and active standing members of the *Audubon Society*, we both figured that birds sleep at night. So we planned to stage the necessary photo op before sundown, master all of our other tasks before sunrise and catch a morning train out of Venice. That's what built-in camera flashes are for right? And besides, have you ever seen a bird fly in the dark of night? Nuff said. This and the troubling logistics of getting there itself, was the entire intellectual foundation of our home stretch racing strategy. Pretty damn impressive, eh?

We had to get to Venice. En route we had to stop off in the picturesque town of Verona, a Mecca of sorts for the incurably romantic. Verona, as local legend suggests, harbors the famous house and balcony of Juliet. Of *Romeo and Juliet* fame. Here, love sick Romeo crooned to his amour, whereby he eventually lowered her vigilant feminine resistance and thus, as the story goes, eventually had his sexual way with her. A lie to be sure. Pure fiction. A myth. No drinks, no dinner, and not even a movie! I don't know any women that simple or easy. Well, maybe just a few. But especially not any Italian women! Talk about low maintenance. It is, by-and-large, yet another cynical attempt at massaging literary history in a vulgar marketing ploy to cash in on tourist trade dollars. Well, actually, cashing in on the *liras*, not the dollars.

I've got to hand it to the local Chamber of Commerce though, their deception seems to have worked. Juliet's balcony is the number one tourist attraction in the city, twenty-five years running! Hey, we were there to see it. I wondered if Shakespeare had any deal points or collected residuals on the back end for his creative writing endeavor? If not, I knew of a good agent at ICM. To set the record straight for those of you that might be fool-hardy enough to attempt to retrace our blazing trail around the world, the famous balcony first appeared in 1921, a historically bad era for tourism in Italy due to the first big war, and the Bard wrote his play "*Romeo and Juliet*" around 1596, give or take a few years. Let's see that's, well…you do the math! We would have attempted to bring this trivial discrepancy of a few centuries up at a Verona City Council meeting, but we simply didn't have the time. Someday though, we vowed to tackle this issue of fraud, along with all the other tourist attraction scams that span the globe. We'll be travel adventure vacation advocates, supporting truth in advertising legislation, while cleaning up pseudo-noteworthy tourist traps. We'll become global Ralph Naders as it were, ferreting out assorted consumer complaints. Or, maybe not.

At any rate, venerable and noble looking Verona was our impending destination. We leapt off the train in this self-proclaimed City of Love at precisely 1:28 p.m. and hailed a cab. We rode in relative comfort to the famous *faux* romantic setting for our obligatory photo-op. It was so romantic that Andy and I embraced ever so briefly, as a couple of blushing Japanese girls on there own pilgrimage to this hallowed sight, snapped our picture. (Actually, we had our hands firmly clasped around each others throats.) Then we scurried through the narrow cobblestone streets past the 22,000 seat *Arena of Verona*, built by the Romans in about 100 CE to a nearby taxi depot. Unknown to us at the time, it was at this point that we once again eluded a potentially lethal fate.

The distinct aroma of rotten eggs filled the air. Bewildered, I cautiously looked at Andy with my eyebrows raised. "Was that you?" I asked with a look of disgust. "No, You?" he quickly retorted. It smelled like something had died nearby.

At that point the local traffic all of a sudden began to remind me of Los Angeles at rush hour in this usually sleepy town of 250,000, as the horns of angered drivers started to wail. While lighting a cigarette, our friendly taxi driver casually informed us that a natural gas pipeline had burst in the center of town. It was a potentially explosive situation. We were somewhat concerned, not wanting to disappear from the face of the earth in a flash as a footnote of history. In reality, our only anxiety was how this touchy situation would effect our well thought out travel plans. Would we make the train to Venice? Were the trains still stopping in Verona? Would we be blown up in the back of a beat up *Fiat* taxi and become nothing more than a mere statistic?

Despite the untimely gas leak, a few extra thousand *lira* got us to the train station on time. The trains were indeed still running, and we departed Verona at exactly 2:11 p.m. Only forty-three minutes after arriving! A new cultural terrorist world record. Wouldn't the boys and girls from the *Guinness* be proud! We were now at the height of our chosen careers: highly skilled professional global grazers.

The last twenty-four hours had been extraordinary. A day full of desperate acts performed by equally desperate men on a desperate mission. Tourist angst had overcome us during this portion of the scavenger hunt from hell. In reality, we weren't like all those other tacky tourists visiting all the must-see sites around the world, one after another, blindly bingeing on history and culture. We were now unequivocally worse. Another of our noble self-imposed myths totally dispelled by our living reality.

Not only that, but our physical appearances were suffering too. We were bordering on that contemporary American homeless chic look: scruffy wrinkled clothes, sweaty bodies, greasy hat-hair and dirty fingernails. Ugh! We had become hideous looking characters. We were nothing more than camera-toting tourists wearing loud Hawaiian shirts and black socks with Bermudas. Pilgrims of the New Age in search of bite-sized morsels of European history and pop-culture. We were now in it for just a quick photo-op. We were no longer the thoughtful, integrated tourists we thought we were in the beginning. The Human*Race* had created two road weary monsters. We had stooped so low we would have been embarrassed with ourselves had it not been for the extreme fatigue that had numbed our usually reliable common sense.

We had however, begun to see the light at the end of this around-the-world ordeal. But we weren't really sure if that light was the dawn of a new day or the sunset of an old one. Or maybe even a nuclear blast on the distant horizon. We might just as well have been in Nepal searching out the legendary *Yeti* in the high Himalayas with a mystical *Sherpa* guide trans-channeling as Dalai Lama Rosenberg. We were lost in the world, missing, but presumed to be having a good time! Totally dazed and confused. Just who was Thomas Cook anyway? Our internal compasses were spinning maniacally out of control. We were victims of a global competition gone seriously awry, and of the money-grubbing travel-industry's sophisticated marketing ploys. With exotic, unique and mysterious destinations quickly whizzing by, 20th Century transportation advances had pushed us boys to the brink of high jinx on the road to somewhere else. It didn't matter anymore where the hell we were. We just were hanging on for the ride. If it was Saturday, and it was exactly 3:13 p.m., then we were surely somewhere on a train between Verona and Venice.

Somehow, while traveling across Europe, we had become a cheap Hollywood composite character. Cast members in yet another *National Lampoon "European Vacation"* movie. Maybe this was all a mere figment of our vivid and now severely distorted imaginations? Maybe we were completely and utterly delirious? Maybe it was nothing more than a collective optical illusion? Totally paranoid by now, we could almost hear the locals whispering amongst themselves, "Who are those guys?" We were committing acts usually reserved for the lowest of sub-humans, GOP political advance men. We had officially gone amok in Europe.

We arrived at Venice's *Santa Lucia* train station at 4 p.m., less than one hour before the cool mid-November sunset. Venice was once a vibrant commercial trading city situated on a lagoon adjacent to the northern end of the Adriatic. Over the centuries, Venetian civilization has attracted the best and brightest of political idealists, along with significant artists of the day. But now, sadly, it seems that Venice is nothing more than a *Disneyland*

with very polluted aromatic canals. Nowadays it only attracts true roman-
tics and misled tourists with disposable income. It has no other function.
In the summer high season over 200,000 tourists a day, more than twice
the local population, tramp and clamor about within the carefully placed
mosaic of about 100 islands. Indeed, Venice would probably not exist at all
today and it would surely have been condemned to urban decay, if it were
not for the daily influx of those touri$t$.

Venice does have a soul though, and can be an enchanting fairytale
land come true on the right day. A beautifully romantic museum cum
tourist attraction bar none. Venice, you see, has a lot to experience: from
its fabulous *palazzi* that line the world famous S-shaped *Canale Grande*,
the narrow labyrinth of cobblestone walkways (There are of course no
cars in Venice.) its many world-class art galleries and other historic
architectural triumphs, the red-brick and white marble walls of *San
Michele* the famous island cemetery, and finally, the majestic splendor
that is *piazza San Marco*. It is the people watching center of the world,
in my mind's eye.

At the very center of Venetian life, the world famous square is surrounded by many treasured galleries, the *Basilica di San Marco*, the famous
clock tower, *Torre dell' Orologio*, scores of charming outdoor cafes, the
impressive *Palazzo Ducale* (Doges Palace), trinket hawkers and the main
Grand Canal itself. You can almost always hear the soft notes of concerto
violins rising in the background, setting a romantic mood for people
watching. It also allows for an unparalleled view of the twin towers of the
Renaissance-era cathedrals of *Chiesa del Redentore* and *San Giorgio
Maggiore*. You're almost tempted to quote a beer commercial: "It just does-
n't get any better than this!" as you sit along the banks of the Grand Canal
watching the sun set over the dome of the *Basilica di Santa Maria della
Salute*. You can wave to the gondola passengers romantically gliding by
with the occasional accordion player and tenor in tow, (For a mere $500
an hour it was reported!?) sipping a bottle of perfection called *Barolo*.
Twilight in Venice is a feast of visual and aural delights as pink and orange

hues, soft harpsichords playing in the background, varied architectural profiles and elegant white marble structures of this floating city, take on a unique life of their own. It certainly has a surreal appeal.

Great Boat Rides
Alaskan Ferry inner passage route
Amsterdam canals
Around Manhattan Island
Canals of Bangkok's Chao Praya River
Seine River Sunset Cruise, Paris
Felecca up the Nile
Ferry up Bosphuras, Istanbul
Greek Inter-Island Ferry
Mandalay to Bagan Irrawaddy River Cruise, Myanmar
Public Water Bus in Venice
San Francisco to Sausalito Ferry
Star Ferry in Hong Kong
Portifino to *Cinque Terre* Ferry, Italy

It was close to dusk when we finally arrived in the busy *Piazza San Marco* via the local *vaporetti* (water bus). We fought our way through unruly throngs of tourists to get to the middle of the *piazza*. The birds were still milling about and all our Venetian tasks were taken care of as the Moorish clock tower rang-out 5 p.m.. We leisurely strolled down narrow pathways, enjoying our time off and a job well done as we located our hotel. Last night I had slept in a French train station luggage locker. Tonight would be a tad different. We both let out a major sigh of relief as we checked into the luxurious five-star *Europa & Regina Hotel*, located on the Grand Canal, knowing a hot shower was in our immediate future. We kept the local switchboard operator hostage for the next hour or so, as trans-Atlantic calls were made to the girlfriends on both the Left and Right coasts of America. The gals back home thought we were missing in action somewhere in the Middle East, for upon our departure they too had no idea where we were headed. Cold German beers, *CNN* on the tube. Incredibly, "*Headline News*" had pictures of the Berlin Wall coming down LIVE! It was pretty emotional. I was sorry that we couldn't head north to Berlin. I really wanted to be there. I was hoping for a last minute scavenge…"A piece of the Berlin Wall!" Historic? Yeah! The *International Herald Tribune* to check in with my Lakers. They had won three in a row! Then long hot showers, turned us ugly road weary tourists into more civilized travelers. A dinner and a movie were the only things missing, aside of course, from the loving girlfriends in this romantic European enclave.

During a long dinner at a relatively inexpensive *trattoria*, which consisted of a bowl of tasty fish soup, mussels, a shared extra cheesy pizza, tenderly breaded veal mozzarella and zesty rigatoni, served with crusty warm bread and a rather mellow bottle of red, (Okay, we had two bottles.) which we discussed our next day's racing strategy. After learning earlier that there were no Monday morning *TWA* flights to New York-Kennedy out of either Vienna or Munich, we decided to make a quick run into Yugoslavia and then double back to Milan, where there was a high noon flight. We figured we'd be in and out of Yugoslavia by mid-afternoon and spend a restful night in Milan. We agreed that the Model Watch program could be reinitiated.

The Human*Race* we concurred, after the second bottle of wine, was ours, and ours alone, to be won. We mentally calculated that we were about eight to twelve hours ahead of the posse because we had gotten to Venice before the sun went down. Remember our Grand rats-with-wings Strategy? In our overly inflated opinions at this time, it was the *TGV* train ride to Chambery and the all-nighter to Milan that made the difference. And that translated into attempting to catch a noon flight on Monday, that we figured, would put us a full day ahead of the pack when we arrived in New York City. Delusions of grandeur or conservative optimism. My glass was half full. Andy's was half empty.

After dinner we indulged in the Saturday night Italian ritual of *passeggiata* through the dramatically lit streets of Venice. Basically, *passeggiata*, like the *paseao* in Spain and cruising in the Valley, is a time for the men and women of the town to casually stroll the streets in the cool crisp Autumn evening air while they flirt amongst each other, and display their finest fall fashions. Coming from a city where you can be arrested and booked for being a pedestrian, the walk was most refreshing. We were getting a lot of pretty intense looks from the locals as we slowly returned to our luxury Grand Canal hotel. We weren't absolutely sure, but it was probably due to one of the following reasons: a) We weren't dressed warmly enough for the brisk evening air; b) We were wearing clothes that should have been burned in Hong Kong some fifteen days ago, or; c) We were extremely drunk and boisterously singing old Cat Stevens songs. The correct answer was, d) All of the above! Nonetheless, we were full of confidence as we retired rather early for a well-deserved *siesta*.

Going Nowhere Fast!

The knock on the door came way too early as the smiling assistant concierge wheeled in the hotel's handy portable heart 'n lung machine practically singing, "Good morning sirs…time to wake up!" How did they know? Perhaps we were just a tad too boisterous returning to the hotel the night before. Even though we'd showered and shaved the night before, we took another extra long one in the morning because by now we had learned that the one constant in this wacky race was that we didn't know where the next one would be. So, as the rhythmic sounds of the heart 'n lung unit emanated from the bedroom, I stood under the hot shower and literally soaked it in, or in it.

As soon as we left the comfort and safety of the hotel the realities of the race smacked us in the face again. First we had to shell out our last 50,000 *lira* for a 6 a.m. *motoscafi* (water-taxi) ride from our Grand Canal perched hotel to nearby *Venice-Santa Lucia* train station. That's fifty bucks for an eight minute ride! Naturally, it was the only eight minute ride available and since we only had ten minutes in which to catch the train, haggling over the price was fruitless. Besides, it was a tax-deductible expense we rationalized again. We hoped to catch the *Simplon-Express*, an adjunct of the world famous *Orient Express* that travels between London and Istanbul, via Yugoslavia.

The Venice-Yugoslavia leg of the renowned train ride is a misnomer if there ever was one. This crowded *SRO* express train took over six and a half hours to travel 120 miles. The problems we encountered during the ride, and there were many of them to report, didn't start to manifest themselves until we got to the town of Trieste, the last town along the Italian-Yugoslavian border. It seemed on this day that it was harder to get into Yugoslavia than it was to cross over the Berlin Wall through *Checkpoint Charlie* from West to East Germany. Wake up and smell the *glasnost* folks. Marshall Tito, aka Josip Broz, died in 1980, remember?

It seemed somewhat symbolic that as we rode a train from Western Europe into Eastern Europe, that the real Iron Curtain was crumbling on that very Sunday morning, November 12th, 1989. The infamous Wall, stretching some 700 miles long, along with its barbed wire fences, trenches, minefields, machine-gun emplacements, vicious guard dogs and highly fortified watchtowers, collectively known as the infamous *strip of death*, were becoming more and more obsolete by the hour. Those husky border guards of the East would be feverishly combing the want ads in the morning. Delirious, freedom-happy, ex-Communist comrades were drinking and dancing wildly to the tunes of *U2* atop the *Brandenburg Gate*. The Wall was now *kaput. Achtung baby*! So what was it that made it so difficult about slipping into, and then slipping out of, semi-socialist Yugoslavia?

The reasons were many: a grossly inefficient transportation system; a slow Sunday schedule; an unfriendly bureaucracy; and finally, acts of absolute stupidity, entirely ours! It would be a stunning lesson in the absurd that we would never ever forget. Just another eighteen hours in the day and life of a couple of global grazers.

After having our now battered and bruised passports thumbed through, checked and severely manhandled, on no less than five separate occasions within an hour by the Yugoslavia border authorities, we felt somewhat secure in our imminent forward progress. We soon learned however, that on the ensuing sixth check, we would be unceremoniously thrown off the train in Sezana to get questionably unnecessary visas officially stamped into our passports. As I recall, there were several AK-47's in evidence, which had the effect of limiting argumentative debate. Of course money was at the heart of the matter. We had officially entered *Document Hell.*

After a brief encounter and exchange with several heavy-set and drab olive green clad *INS*-types, our passports were stamped. The tourist visa we received looked a lot like a Westwood parking lot validation stamp. The officials signaled us back on board the waiting train. We emerged from the station house to find a restless crowd of passengers glaring at us through the train's windows. We shrugged our shoulders and apologetically bowed to the other passengers hoping we wouldn't be mugged when the journey resumed. Looking at the people you had the feeling they were thinking, "Jesus, another couple of arrogant Americans presuming that their little blue passport excuses them from paperwork!" And they would have been right...

It became apparent early on that they liked order here. A lot of order. And, after the last couple of weeks on the road, we were an unsightly duo not to be trusted. Either that, or, they didn't fully appreciate the "Tito, the Great Unifier was alive!" rumor we had started earlier in the day on the train. We had been making jokes with everybody who could understand English, that we had recently seen The Great Dictator at a Paris *McDonald's*! He was working behind the counter. No one laughed though?! Andy checked to see if the microphone was plugged in.

But then again, the Yugoslavians have always had an identity crisis of sorts. Their mountainous country of twenty-four million is a rather loose, emphasis on the word loose, post-World War I creation of eight radically different confederated republics. And to make matters worse, it has no less than five distinct ethnic groups, four separate commonly used languages, three official state religions, Eastern-Orthodox, Roman Catholic and Islamic, along with two working alphabets, Latin and Cyrillic. All of these entities co-exist in an area about the size of Oregon. Talk about a civil war waiting to happen! The term *Lebanonization,* I predict, will have great meaning in Yugoslavia in the very near future.

Called the Land of the Southern Slavs, the friendly Yugoslavian people have always had a tough time with historical and geographic delineations. In the 4th Century, with the Roman Empire breaking up, the dividing line between the Byzantine (East) and the all new and improved Holy Roman Empire (West) went right through the middle of this Balkan peninsula. A thousand years later, it became the dividing line again between the Turkish Ottoman Empire (East) and the Christian-Hapsburg Empire (West). And finally, after World War II, and six-centuries of Austrian rule, it became the Iron Curtain dividing line. Actually Yugoslavia was a member of the so-called Non-Aligned Nations, siding with neither NATO nor the Warsaw Pact officially. But you never heard that in our press. In the continual historic *do-si-do* change of shifting international alliances, Yugoslavia it seems has always been reluctantly caught in the middle. What can I say, this country is one big DMZ. Rudyard Kipling was right when he declared that "East is East and West is West, and never the twain shall meet." Okay, I know the quote was applied to Kipling's India-British dichotomy, but hey, it's apt here too!

Our visit was taking us to the northern-most region of Yugoslavia, the ex-Republic of Slovenia. They are a somewhat free and independent state, although under the watchful eye of the Austrian rulers until 1918, when it freely elected to join with the other Slavic states into what is modern day Yugoslavia. Its two million residents, 87% Slovene, are mostly industrious Roman Catholics, in a country of mixed ethnic and religious denominations. This particular region, which represents only eight percent of Yugoslavia's entire population, more than adequately pulls its own economic weight by producing over twenty percent of the nation's GDP and over a quarter of the central government's bloated budget. And with its close ties to the European Community, it produces over thirty percent of the nation's hard currency earnings.

We arrived in Postojna, a cute, sleepy little town of six thousand, and the first of our two Yugoslavian destinations, by early afternoon. We hadn't completed any of our tasks yet and we were already running severely behind schedule.

Our objective here was to visit the famous caves of Postojna (*Postojnska Jama*), and to do so we had to brush up on our college speleology classes. Look that one up in your *Funk and Wagnalls*! Who knew there was even such a place as the Postojna caves? We ended up spending more time in these cold, dark and lonely, four million year old caves than we did in *gay Paree*! Edward, our enthusiastic and highly informative English speaking tour guide, masterfully led us through the fantastic rock formations and labyrinthine passages to our required photo-op destination. He livened up, what we imagined was his usually insipid cave commentary, with a few off-color jokes for Andy and I. We then had our picture taken in front of a *stalactite* called the Brilliant Column. Or maybe it was a *stalagmite*? We took a group photo with Edward at our side smiling gleefully. It would make a good postcard we thought. Then we had to find some type of weird amphibian that they had on exhibit. A *proteus anguineus*, that they had inaccurately named the "Human Fish." We quickly found the little milky-white four legged genetic mutant that allegedly had a life span of over seventy years, and escaped from this depressing cave.

Postojnska Jama, we had learned from Edward, was discovered in 1818. No doubt by a founding affiliated member of the National Speleological Society (NSS). The Germans had briefly used the cave as both a prison and a bomb shelter-like storage facility for their armored tank petroleum reserves. We left the Nazi prison camp cum tourist attraction in order to catch yet another, loosely-defined, express train to the interior of Yugoslavia.

The train was called the *Ljubljana Express*. A more apt namesake, I thought, would have been the *Gypsies, Tramps and Thieves Local*. Historical myths, State Department disinformation and friendly travel advice alike, lead me, now fearing the worst, to ever so vigilantly watch our belongings as we traveled through the mountainous autumn countryside. The train, more like an old Chicago *El* subway car, was packed with fellow travelers en route to Ljubljana. Most were on their way to Belgrade, the nation's capital. It would have been a long snail's paced ride to Belgrade on this particular day, I thought to myself. The combination of dark hair and facial features, ragged clothing, shifty dark piercing eyes, dirty hands covered by fingerless gloves, and dozens of children, made me wonder about gypsy legends coming true. They deviously eyeballed the two of us. Then laughed. They then wishfully scrutinized our couple of bags. Then secretively plotted amongst themselves. They shrewdly checked out the closest train exits. Then calculatingly eyeballed our bags once again. Or so my paranoid mind was saying! We became, oh, just a tad nervous, as this imaginary conspiracy unfolded right before our overly paranoid eyes.

Nothing happened that evening on the *Ljubljana Express*. Nothing usually ever does. But our tired, yet vivid imaginations had once again gotten the best of us. We should have been singing Hungarian gypsy songs and handing out the sugarless *Wrigley's* chewing gum to the kids. But instead we were questioning the basic human nature of these simple peasants.

We were entering the final days of our around-the-world travel adventure odyssey, day sixteen to be exact. The last of our foreign scavenges awaited us. We had come too far to screw up now. Precaution was in the air. Our gypsies-on-a-crime-spree fears quickly faded, dissolving once again into a collective optical illusion.

As if in some low budget World War II spy movie, a thick fog greeted us as we arrived at our destination. It created a sense of foreboding eeriness as we embarked on our errands in this Cold War Eastern European town. The dark outlines of steep roofs, huge cathedral domes and church spires took on vague shapes. Out of the pages of a cheap spy novel, Ljubljana, a Balkan town nearing its two thousandth birthday, was a place where foreign intrigue could possibly thrive, at least in our now sugar deficient fertile imaginations. It oozes with an air of faded

Austro-Hungarian-Baroquean elegance, with slight tinges of Counter-Reformation-Retro-Italian influences mixed in for good measure. The Hapsburgs were a really big hit here! We actually had no idea how the city looked. It was foggy and we were totally blinded by exhaustion. We did know for sure that it was late Sunday evening, and that most of this town of three hundred thousand was home watching "*Murder She Wrote*." All the bars, terrace cafes, pizzerias and grills near *Preseren Square* were closed. However, it seemed like business as usual near the combination train/bus station in the city center. We were told that a magnificent 12th Century medieval fortress-castle called *Grad*, overlooked the whole town from a hill. "Maybe next time?" I informed a hustling tour guide.

Our first priority was to negotiate for a cab. Usually not a difficult task under normal circumstances. But normal circumstances had long since passed us by ten days ago crossing Java. Nothing would ever be normal again after this. To make matters worse, we didn't have any more of that funny looking Yugoslavian currency. Oh, we weren't by any means poor. A direct violation of *Commandment No. 1*! Nor would we be forced to beg, borrow or sell ourselves in the cold mean streets of Ljubljana. We had all kinds of money; French *francs,* Hong Kong dollars, Indonesian *rupiahs, American Express* Travelers checks, Polish *zlotys* left over from a previous trip, and even Eskimo *pence*. But we had already spent our last two million Yugo *dinars* on lunch, beers in Postojna, cave fees and train tickets. We couldn't locate a handy money-changer anywhere. And Andy can bare witness to the fact that I couldn't find any of those notoriously convenient ATM cash machines in the immediate vicinity. No one would cash my *Eurocheck* anywhere. It was clear that the incredible shrinking dollar had reeked havoc on our personal finances. It was an uncomfortable non-liquid economic situation. You try hiring a cab at LAX and telling the cabby, before sitting down, in his warm comfy taxi, that you're going to have to pay your fare with Malaysian *ringgitts* or Egyptian pounds. It ain't gonna happen, is it folks?

Luckily for us, the Europeans are a little more financially flexible in situations like this. Especially in Eastern Europe. They're more, shall we say, Continental? Cash is cash. Most any currency will usually do. Switzerland is but a stone's throw away. Unless of course you're carrying a pocketful of those unconvertible Russian *rubles*, or those ever so hard to explain *EMU's* and *SDR's*. They do however tend to get a bit touchy when you pull out the pocket calculator in an attempt to figure out a more favorable exchange rate. We had to be creative. So I handed the driver one of our disposable $19.95 *Swatch Watch's* that we used occasionally in these types of situations. It usually works. We waited for his approval. It was a done deal. No further questions were asked and we were on our way.

Our first stop was the famous *Dragon Bridge*. We talked the taxi driver into taking a quick photo of us shivering in the cold dark fog with the dragon-like gargoyles, guarding this medieval passage over the Ljubljanica River. It took us a whole five or six seconds. Remember, we are professionals.

By now it was getting later and there was a minor concern brewing between Andy and I about getting out of Yugoslavia in time to catch an early morning flight to New York City. Ah, New York City! It seemed so distant. This day had not gone as smoothly as we had planned over dinner the night before in Venice. We finally arrived at *Robba's Fountain*, our second and final local HumanRace destination, only to find it all boarded up. Protection from the harsh winter that seemed to be blowing in as we stood there. Our next image, was a wild and crazy one, yet not entirely unexpected, for the HumanRace. We had come to expect the wholly unexpected.

There we were, on a Sunday evening in front of a boarded up fountain in the middle of an exotic looking East European town called Ljubljana. Suddenly, out of the dense foggy night two guys appear, running wildly through the cold barren cobblestone streets heading in our direction. We were a little taken aback by this rapidly approaching sight. Our cautious internal *IFF* radar systems were already overtaxed beyond repair. Then, to our complete and utter surprise, we discovered that it was Mitchell and Kevin. Two fellow racers who had become good comrades with us along the way.

"What are you guys doing?" we asked, giving each other friendly bear hugs. They had been stranded in town and had taken a room for the night at the assigned hotel. They had also been drinking heavily. "Train schedules and cave tour hours that we couldn't quite make." was Mitchell's slurred reply. Together we quickly had a group photo of us taken in front of the hidden Robba Fountain. Official documentation of us being there together in the last days of this heated competition. A treasured memento of Yugoslavia.

A brief discussion ensued about the viability of tearing down the few plywood sheets covering this ancient fountain, but it was the liquor talking and the idea was quickly rebuffed by cooler heads. Yugoslavian jails were not my idea of a good time. We spoke about joining them for a few cognacs at a nearby cafe, when just as quickly as they materialized, they disappeared. As their yelling and maniacal laughter faded, Andy and I were left standing in thick fog, looking into gray nothingness. "Yugoslavia will do that to you," one of us noted. Shrugging our shoulders, we hopped into our warm taxi. It was fun while it lasted. Just another surrealistic global encounter to be sure. We would have to wait until we were all in New York to see just how this bizarre episode ended.

Getting to New York City itself was gonna prove to be yet another logistical challenge. As I mentioned before, originally we had planned to depart from Vienna, Austria, but after some wisely placed telephone calls, we learned that there weren't any Monday morning flights out of Vienna. Plan B, for *BAD*, was immediately thrown into action. We now had to double back to Milan in order to catch a noon *TWA* flight. If we missed that plane we'd have to cool our heels a full day before the next one departed. At which point we would officially become time bankrupt. It could mean the difference between winning and losing this debacle of a race. Needless to say, off we went, *post haste*, in the direction of Venice. But how were we going to achieve this feat we wondered? We had less than twelve hours to figure it out.

After sitting and reflecting on our plight in an extremely smoky Ljubljana train station cafe for the better part of an hour sucking down recycled coffee, we boarded an 11 p.m. train headed for Italy. Unfortunately, it was only headed towards Italy. It was not actually going to enter Italy, let alone Milan. We would have to disembark in Sezana. It would not be going the rest of the way into Italy until 6 a.m. the following morning. We couldn't wait that long. We would have to get across the Italian-Yugo border some other way. The train conductor waved us off the train a short hour later. We still didn't quite know what we were going to do. A rabbit would have to be pulled out of the proverbial hat. And soon!

At the Sezana train station waiting room, more like a stuffy picture-lined hallway actually, we found no one waiting around and no railroad personnel from which to seek out vital information. We had no one to seek counsel from. We had no one to bribe. The town was seemingly closed for the night. It was Sunday after all, and not all communists are atheists we unfortunately learned. There wasn't even a road nearby to hitch hike on, no buses to book passage on, and definitely no taxis. We spotted a small smoke-filled cafe nearby and took refuge. No luck there, mostly barflies. What were we gonna do?

We stood around freezing for a few moments contemplating our impending doom. It looked very bleak indeed. Our options? Hell we had no options! We needed divine intervention. Just then, a tall dark athletic looking man came out of the shadows heading towards an Italian sports car parked in the parking lot. We confronted him in a butchered Slovene dialect and naturally didn't even get a hint of recognition from him. I myself, take pride in the fact that I've been to scores of countries around the world, and am still a dissident monolingual speaking American. Andy, on the other hand, speaks more languages than *Berlitz* has tapes, but apparently not Slovenian. This was one of those times I would've died for a stupid quickie phrase book. But no such luck. We were, after all, traveling extremely light.

Steely-eyed glances are all that came from the man, until Andy tried his luck in Italian. It worked. We had communication. Introductions were quickly made. His name was Nico. Nico listened to our plight with a furrowed brow and a cocked head. Eventually, he offered us his personal assistance. He'd drive us to Trieste, on the Italian side of the border. From there we would be on our own. We were overjoyed. I was getting sicker by the minute and it was getting really nippy outside. Not to mention the fact that our race clock was ticking like a time bomb ready to explode in twelve short hours. We crammed into the small two seater and just as we were ready to go, a convoy of Yugoslavian Military Police vehicles arrived on the scene and pulled into the parking lot. It was like a scene out of a bad movie. A really bad movie.

After a lengthy and animated discussion, we seemed to have gotten ourselves out of any legal difficulties. That good old US Passport will do it every time. Especially when you have a freshly folded twenty dollar bill hidden inside it! It did however take our new found friend, Nico, several more painstaking minutes to get himself out of harms way. Spies, smuggling documents, currency violations, cavorting with undesirables, soon-to-be-expired passports and those colorful Palestinian head dresses we had in our bags, seemed to be the major topics of discussion. Or so we imagined. We stood by quietly, wanting very much to intercede on Nico's behalf. But ever so diplomatically, we quietly stood shivering in the now frigid cold midnight air. Finally, Nico's persuasive hand and facial gesturing won them over somehow and we were on our way along the *autoput*. We were making a run for the border.

Getting into Italy was no problem. It was leaving Yugoslavia that once again proved to be the real challenge. We thought they were probably worried about a brain drain taking place. Dalmatians running for freedom, or maybe they feared capital flight with their *dinar* zooming off to secret Swiss bank accounts. Or maybe they're concerned about people exporting some of their well-made specialty products, like their *Yugo* automobiles. At any rate, we had yet another diplomatic delay as we dealt with the Yugoslavian Customs and Immigration officers. After finally giving us permission to leave, the Italians just waved us on through. They didn't care. Apparently they're not too worried about what comes out of Yugoslavia. So much for the Cold War invasion myths.

Andy started talking with Nico about his life, family and personal interests as he sped down the highly efficient Italian Adriatic Highway that goes some 650 miles from the middle of Italy to the Albanian coast. At this point we were attempting to disarm Nico. Win him over in the hope of his good nature working further in our favor. Simply put, we didn't want to be stranded at 2 a.m. in the sleepy town of Trieste, Italy, for even a few minutes, let alone till daylight. After learning that he was a professional truck driver, and that he had no less than three different girlfriends, all of whom lived in separate cities, Venice, Rome and Milan, we touched on the topic of sports. That seemed to liven him up and talk of basketball, specifically the Los Angeles *Lakers* totally won him over. Magic, Kareem, Worthy, Michael Cooper and the new kid from Yugoslavia of all places, Vlade Divac, really got him on a roll. So much so that we pulled over at the next truck stop so that he could make a quick phone call, as Andy and I plotted to ply him with piping hot *expresso*. "*Rapido! Rapido! A tutta velocita!*" we joked with him. We were no longer going nowhere fast.

Nico came through for us; he would take us all the way to Venice after all. We thanked him over and over again offering candy, petrol, *lira*, anything in sincere gratitude. Nico smiled knowingly, declining all of our offers of thanks. "But me want your address." he said in broken English. "If me come to LA, me want to see the *Lakers* beat those bad boy *Pistons*." he smiled. "Guaranteed Nico!" I replied happily, as I handed him my business card. "A pre-game dinner at *Fatburgers* too," I added. He smiled and off we went at 150 kilometers an hour.

We were going to make that noon flight to New York departing from Milan after all. But we learned a lot on this side trip. What we thought was going to be a quick little foray into Yugoslavia, turned into an eighteen hour marathon episode out of Rod Serling's "*The Twilight Zone*."

We said our *arrivedercis* to Nico in the industrial town of Mestre, a quick six minute train ride from the canals of Venice. He dropped us after a three hour drive into the wee small hours of the night. Finding an Italian version of a *Motel 6* in the vicinity of the train station was no problem. Although the nameless hotel we checked into was functional if utterly charmless, it could have been a wonderful living final exam question for UCLA's School of Hotel Administration on how *not* to run a hotel! Much too tired to fill out the customer service questionnaire we finally caught some needed shut eye after an embarrassing and humbling long day.

We had about four hours to sleep before the 7 a.m. train to Milan. It would be a three hour ride to *Milan's Central Station*, followed by an hour or so taxi ride out to *Malpensa International Airport*. Theoretically, we figured, that we should make that noon flight to New York with, oh, an hour or so to spare.

Lawyers, Guns and Money in New York City

What was supposed to be a restful, subdued and somewhat reflective flight back to New York City as possible first place contenders of the inaugural Human*Race*, turned out to be our worst nightmare come true. To set the tone for the entire day, we barely made the train, let alone our plane. In fact, after the three hour train ride and a longer-than-we-thought ninety dollar cab ride to the airport, we had the thoughtful Italian ground crew actually push the *TWA* L-1011 bound for JFK back to its loading gate. How we conducted this amazing feat I'm not at liberty to say. I'm sworn to secrecy. But a fact is a fact. Something about a visit from Mr. Ben Franklin! Breathless, we scurried up the stairs to enter the awaiting jet.

What an entrance it was too. What an unmitigated disaster. What a blow to our egos. What a party!

On board already, securely tucked into their assigned seats, wearing their seat belts and listening to Mozart's *Piano Quartet in E major* over the jet's stereo system, were no less than four other racing teams. We were stunned. It was a body blow beyond compare. Officially speaking, they were all equally depressed at seeing our surprised faces on board that plane. For they all knew that we were quite possibly the potential front runners at this juncture of the Human*Race*.

To their credit though, they all slapped our backs in a friendly competitive way and warmly, albeit, baffled by our sudden appearance, welcomed us aboard. The camaraderie at this point was overwhelming. Here we had just spent the last seventeen days ferociously playing a wacky game of

"*Beat the Clock*" around-the-world against these very people and now everyone realized that it all came down to but a flip of the coin as to just who would win this insane ordeal. Andy and I looked at each other in total disbelief. We were one step away from tears. And not tears of joy. The flight attendants frantically ushered us into our seats. I stared into never-never-land trying to figure out just what had happened. Question's abounded: *How? Why? When? Where? What?* and *Who?* Followed by the traditional: *Coulda! Shoulda! Woulda! Buts!*

Let it be noted that Andy said all along that, "We are not BIG men yet…" He said he had a funny feeling and even though he tried to put away the thoughts and go with my optimistic mood, he had a funny feeling we were in for a surprise. Turns out it was more like four surprises! So, by the time we staggered onto the plane, he too was convinced that we had pulled off a major coup. I even allowed myself to imagine that maybe, just maybe, we had done it. WHAM! No way Jose.

The usual suspects had been rounded up for the flight home. Kevin and Mitchell were on board. Now we knew why they didn't share a late night drink with us in Ljubljana just twelve short hours ago. Now we also knew why they were laughing hysterically as they ran down the cobble-stoned street into the cold and foggy Yugoslavian night. They had a plan in their wackiness.

Bill and Mike, the able Del Ray Boys were on board also, though obviously not real happy to see us at this point. They looked extremely worse for wear. Upon further inquiry, we learned that they hadn't slept in a hotel since Cairo, almost four long days ago! We too had spent a restless night sleeping in a train station luggage locker, but, we also had two, albeit short night's sleep in clean, white sheeted beds. On the road for over eighty hours, the boys seemed to have gotten the job done, but the hard way.

Also on board were Wayne and Enid. A spunky unmarried middle-aged couple from Park Ridge, Illinois. Although basically out of the running, due to a few technical violations concerning some alleged unauthorized activities during the Southeast Asian segment, the fact that they were on board hurt our professional pride to no end. Later, we found out that they had blown off whole sets of the assigned scavenges. It helped ease my pain a little.

And finally, Terry and Susan, from Madison, Indiana were present and accounted for. They were smiling those big smiles that we came to basically understand during the course of the race as, "Howdy boys...we look like rubes but underneath these suburban disguises lie competitive hearts like you've never seen." Either that or, "Nanner, nanner, nanner! We're here too!" We sat in our seats across the aisle from them. The looks on their respective faces hinted that they had almost pulled off a major *coup*.

The events that had just taken place called for an early afternoon snort or two, or three, or four. I sat back and plugged in my stereo headset blocking out the world for a few minutes. Nothing clears the head like Jimi Hendrix at 35,000 feet. I gazed out my window and looked down over the geo-sphere in which we live, as we crossed over the snow capped Swiss Alps. I soaked in a full 3.25 *milliseiverts* (*mSv*) dose of cosmic radiation as we flew to a higher altitude. We were finally homeward bound...

The plane took a sweeping right hand turn and descended from the heavens through billowy white clouds. It was a cold, drizzling and dreary day. Welcome to New York. Home of the Brave. We were temporary exiles returning home. We had made it. We were home. But first we had to answer to those nasty US Customs officers with zero tolerance for anything.

The US Customs office must be an interesting place to work. I can almost envision a hit TV sitcom taking place here. Complete with situation-comedy ensemble cast, ala *"Barney Miller"* with the following players: A gung-ho pudgy Hispanic woman who hand searches Italian nuns; the recently transferred laid-back California supervisor; the suave politically ambitious night school law student; the sarcastic lifelong civil servant who's seen everything and everybody; and of course, Murphy the temperamental drug sniffing K-9 member of the staff. What a supporting cast of thousands too, jet-lagged, harried and contraband-laden tourists passing through these gates, all of course claiming that they've got *"Nothing to Declare!"*

After pitching Andy on my idea as we waited in line, he gave me a blank stare then rambled something about me spending way too much time in La-La Land taking meetings in Burbank, doing lunch in Century City and thinking seriously about prime time television. Said I needed a support group that offers a 12-step program, like SA, *Screenwriters Anonymous.*

Our passports now looked like a messy coloring book with all the different entry and exit visa stamps that had been pounded into them over the last three weeks. A traveler takes a certain amount of pride in his official visa stamp collection. They're like battlefield ribbons. I know people who actually ask wholly indifferent Immigration agents to please stamp their passports for posterity. Officer A. Henderson zipped through my passport quickly asking me the question I longed to hear, "How many months have you been out of the USA?" I smiled a knowing smile and looked right at him responding, "Seventeen days, sir! Not quite three weeks." He looked at me with a certain degree of bewilderment as he quickly perused my dog-eared and tattered passport once again. With one word he said it all, *"Explain!"*

I became increasingly nervous as our encounter moved along, but for no apparent reason. I really did have nothing to declare. But a past memory made me feel a tad paranoid. The Cold War era did that to some people. You see, it all started back in 1985, when Andy and I traveled to Thailand for a couple of days. The US Customs Service, ever suspicious of my unusual travel patterns, created a file on me. I became a data entry member of the Fed's so-called *"Lookout List."* (Not to be confused with the INS's *"Watch List"* that attempts to make sure hardened criminals, political terrorists and billions of anti-Reagan dissidents alike, aren't allowed to enter the country.) I was erroneously pegged as either a gun-runner, money launderer, narcotics trafficker, high-tech contraband smuggler, subversive or Eastern-bloc spy. Wrong on all accounts of course. I am now however an admitted terrorist, albeit, a cultural one. I must admit that at first I kind of liked the romantic aspect of being under suspicion by the mighty US Government and enjoyed the subterfuge and intrigue created by it all. It made for engrossing conspiratorial conversation at diplomatic dinner parties and impressed the hell out of my travel dates with all that extra attention I got every time I came back into the country. But ever since then, whenever I come back to my native place of birth I get the third degree while the officer glimpses at his blinking iridescent green computer screen revealing highly personal data about me.

I'm absolutely convinced, though it may indeed be nothing more than complete paranoia on my part, that the file is filled with intensely embarrassing personal information. Like, that I once failed Sociology 1A, *yes Soc 1A!*, in high school. Or that I was once arrested for underage drinking in Canada. Or that I once purchased some of that anti-balding cream while wearing a yellow fedora at a neighborhood *Savon* drug store. Or that I emptied a few hotel mini-bars without paying? I thought that maybe, after all these years of being a responsible, civic-minded and free man, that maybe they had pictures of me tossing that thirty-two ounce cup of beer at that cop more than a decade ago during a wild melee in the centerfield bleachers of *Tiger Stadium*. Or maybe, I speculated wildly, they somehow knew about that brief trans-Atlantic liaison with that bushy-haired suicidal manic-depressive flight attendant who wavered between her role models of Mother Teresa and Lady Di along the Adriatic Coast of Yugoslavia and Napa Valley. Looking into my skeleton closet always freaks me out a little. It's where I store all my old unwanted baggage. And it's probably better off kept there too, ignored, safe, dark and isolated. Repressed memories. Relics of my past...

Quickly though, while all these past random transgressions bounced around in my head, I brashly said to him with a certain amount of pride,

"Well you see officer I was involved in an around-the-world scavenger hunt…" He abruptly cut me off with, "Oh, one of those." And then he quickly added, "Go ahead. Next!" returning my passport and waving me on. I was a little taken aback by his, "Oh, one of those!" comment. And was equally hurt that I wasn't able to fully explain to a fellow American my recent misadventures of a lifetime. It would have to wait.

Andy was waving at me to hurry up, having already cleared US Customs. For some reason he doesn't have his name in the data file. And I'm somewhat suspicious about that too.

Our only task at this point was to quickly get to the nearby *Holiday Inn at the Airport* to officially check in and stop our race clock. Now the fun really began.

The irony of it all. Here we had just circumnavigated the globe. Effectively dealt with just about any and every crazy situation that one can confront while on the road abroad. We had survived a train fire in the searing Egyptian desert, exploding volcanoes in the prehistoric jungles of Java, we, er, I had survived deadly pit vipers wrapped around my neck, all night bus rides through dense tropical rain-forests; we had dined with a prince and had been treated like royalty at numerous banquets held in our honor all around the globe, we had communicated in at least a dozen different dialects to scores of train conductors, *bemo* and *tuk-tuk* drivers, rickshaw peddlers, ferry-boat captains, ox-cart drivers, camel jockeys, and an ethnically diverse host of taxi-cab drivers, but we hadn't survived New York City yet. New York is always a humbling experience.

Surprise! Our New York cabby didn't speak a word of English. And between Andy and I, we spoke not a word of what we thought was Haitian!? We yelled. We panicked. We cajoled. We cursed. And we yelled some more. He didn't know where the hell the fucking hotel was, let alone how to get us there from here. Furthermore, he acted as if he just didn't give a shit and was gonna eventually drop us off in midtown Manhattan someplace after a $50 fare. We all but jumped out of the speeding taxi as it neared the proximity of the hotel. It was a long perilous journey of three miles via the gridlocked Van Wyck Expressway. The hotel itself was always within visual sight from the moment we left the terminal. It was getting there that was the real problem. We finally made it into the lobby as the electronic media shone it's ever-so-bright lights upon us. Andy was livid. If timing hadn't been so crucial it might have been comical. I wasn't in much better shape, completely spent after seventeen days of dealing. All of the others who had been on the plane with us had already checked-in and stopped their respective race clocks.

I could almost see it now: "Valvur and Chalmers place second in the First Annual Human*Race*, losing the around-the-world race by three minutes to the first place finishers of…"

After finally checking in that Monday afternoon, Andy went to his comfy apartment on the upper Westside to get reacquainted with his live-in girlfriend. I on the other hand spent the next three days ordering room service, listening to jet engines, sleeping eighteen hours a day and attempting to nurse myself back to health. An unhealthy combination of sheer exhaustion from the extended trip, not eating properly for a few weeks and a nasty little Yugo cold bug, had left me totally and utterly incapacitated. The results of the race were to be announced on Friday after all the other stragglers had returned from their European vacation. I, for one, could wait.

By Thursday I was feeling somewhat chipper again after three days of isolation in the intensive care ward of the Airport Holiday Inn. I stayed hunkered down in the Howard Hughes suite. Andy and I met a friend at the art deco-styled *Cafe Iguana* in Manhattan for lunch. It was here that Andy and I recovered from our collective memory hole, although we were both still a little groggy after our trip. Our jaded view of things was still present in our slurred speech patterns. My girlfriend flew in from Los Angeles to help me in my healing process. We later met up with all the other Human*Racers* who had just returned home. Several teams were missing in action and were probably still having fun in

Europe. Some had just gone home having had enough of the whole road experience for the time being.

A lot of idle speculation as to who the winners were was taking place in the hotel lobby bar. Several team members were seen mounting intensive lobbying campaigns with the scoring officials, jockeying for better positions. Remember what was at stake here: lucrative book contracts, talk show appearances, ego and lots of cold hard cash! All this rested in the balance of the final outcome. Nasty charges and counter-charges of whole scale cheating and unfair advantages were openly and passionately debated. Points were made. Counterpoints were made. The threat of a lawsuit was mentioned. *Civil court I believe it was*. We tried to stay out of the fray as much as we possibly could. We clearly had our own logic as to how the scoring ought to have been conducted. But then again, we had already decided way back in Singapore, that JB's crack staff were way too sophisticated for us. All we knew for sure was that we had done everything that was asked of us. We had completed all 106 scavenges (Except of course for the two false leads in Chambery and Luxor.) and had finished the global course extremely fast. We had survived the race both politically and ethically unscathed in our fellow participants and the organizers' eyes. Everybody in the racing group had more or less taken a shine to us by this point for some reason. Maybe it was our detached air. Maybe our self-confidence. Who knew? But as far as we were concerned, our future looked so bright we had to wear shades.

Another media orgy was called for on Friday at 3 p.m. at the *Marriott Marquis* in Times Square. Cameras and flashes clicked in synchronized orgasmic bliss. Fame, fortune and a crystal trophy awaited one of the seventeen teams left competing. But first, we would have to survive JB's last chance at completely humiliating us for the benefit of the corporate sponsors in front of the local media. It was to be a real dog and pony show par excellence. We would have to race through, up and down Manhattan, and perform a handful of odd-ball scavenges. David

Letterman has the correct name for these merciless feats we were about to perform and aptly refers to them as "*Stupid Human Tricks.*"

We were given our final set of assignments at 8 a.m. sharp. Off the teams went quickly scattering into the bright and crisp autumn morning in the New York urban jungle. Aside from completing all the required scavenges themselves, the only rule was that we were specifically prohibited from taking any cabs. Shit, how was JB gonna enforce this rule. Some team members actually flew across Java and were summarily slapped on the wrist for their transgression. What was he gonna do if you hailed a cab for a few city blocks? We understood the spirit of JB's commandments. So the subway, buses and walking were to be our alternative modes of transportation for the next few hours. There was a certain amount of consistency to his edict.

Like all of our destinations in the past, we took the city by storm. From *Grant's Tomb*, ironically the first time either Andy or I had ever seen it, to *Poe's Cottage*. We fought with the morning rush hour commuters. In a famed New York minute, we took photos of us visiting the Met, Wall Street's *Fraunces Tavern*, and the architecturally historic Downtown *Flat Iron Building*. We had a bagel with lox at *Zabar's Deli*, had a hot-dog with the works at Lower East Side *Katz's Delicatessen* on East Houston, scene of Meg Ryan's fake orgasm in "*When Harry Met Sally,*" and stole some matches from the Midtown *Russian Tea Room*. We checked out the menu at *Umberto's Clam House* in Little Italy where Joey Gallo bought the farm. "Who's Joey Gallo?" I kept asking over and over again without ever getting a response. And before you could say three-card monte, we found *Cleopatra's Needle* in the infamous Muggers Paradise, Central Park.

Before we could finish the urban race course however, we had to either visit *Coney Island* or the top of the *Statue of Liberty*. We chose the oversized bronze goddess. It was all a matter of timing we concluded once again. The ferry left for the island on the hour and departed from the island on the half hour. Joining us on the ferry was Kevin and

Mitchell. We collectively talked about our strategy. Bud Collins, the white bearded *CBS Sports* tennis analyst overheard our conversation and thought we were certifiably nuts. We filled him in on the goings-on of the last couple of weeks of the global Human*Race*. Stunned, he nodded his head, seemingly now understanding our peculiar plight. I was still a tad under the weather, and Mitchell had hurt his leg earlier, so we were both out of action. It was up to Andy and Kevin to jump off the ferry, race to the crown at the top, take a picture as proof they were there, and get back on the boat before the half hour departure time. They had twelve minutes to complete the task.

Bud, always the sports commentator said, "No way guys." We told Bud to hang around and witness a true act of sporting madness. It wouldn't be the first time that good old Bud would be wrong, he's also picked Ivan Lendl to win at *Wimbledon* for the last five years. *He's oh-for…*

The very second the boat docked, before it was even tied up, the two brave lads leaped to the sidewalk with a running start. Bud, Mitchell and I watched in delight. The clock was now ticking. They had twelve minutes. The ferry boat would quickly unload and just as quickly reload for the trip back to the city. Mitchell and I formulated a ground strategy. He would fall to the ground, faking a broken leg or something on the gang plank, to buy some extra minutes if necessary. I would meet the boys at the base of Lady Liberty, and urge them on, or signal Mitchell if it was necessary for him to stall. *Ten minutes to go…*Bud bought us a couple of hot black coffees while the three of us waited in anticipation. The three of us had some time for casual small talk.

They started to reload the ferry with passengers for the trip back to Manhattan. *Five minutes to go…*Mitchell and I put plan A into effect.

I waited and waited for Kevin and Andy to materialize from the base of Miss Liberty. No sight of them. *Three minutes to go…*the ferry's whistle blows again. *Two minutes to go…*nothing yet? I was beginning to get nervous. Confident in our plan, but uncertain as to its eventual outcome. *One minute to go…*then out of the dark hall leading from the stairwell I see them running towards me. I signal Mitchell to start his act. I frantically waved them over to me. Their jackets are off. Their sweaters are off. Their shirts are hanging out. They're sweating terribly and breathing extremely hard. Andy looks pale. Kevin is very red in the face. And all I could say was, "Dr. Livingston I presume."

Thirty seconds to go... we get to the dock as Bud gives us an ovation and yells out some words of encouragement. Everybody was thumbs up! The ferry boat crew, now fully aware of Andy and Kevin's feat, waved us on with a loud cheer. The whistle blows. We jump on the ferry as the passengers looked at us with strange unknowing glares. Andy immediately falls to the ground. I really thought he was going to have a coronary. Looking at me, you'd have thought he was a man trying to physically exhale a lung. But they had made it. We had survived the ordeal. We finished the Human*Race*.

A little CPR and a cold brew and the boys were both all right. Their tale was one of frenzied actions, constant yelling, "Coming up!" then, "Coming down!" and a mutual, wholly understandable fear of certain heart failure. Now New York City had an unofficial record to break. Up and down the *Statue of Liberty* in twelve minutes. Go ahead, give it a try.

We marched on back to the midtown *Marriott Marquis* together and entered the banquet room arm in arm showing the solidarity of our common bond. The area was full of reporters, photographers, corporate sponsors' representatives and smiling loved ones. The Del Ray Boys had beaten us back by a few minutes and it was fingernail chewing nervous time in New York. Despite the confidence we had displayed throughout the entire race, we were never really certain as to our official standing. Were we a respectable third or fifth in the running? Could we have possibly won the race? The race organizers were being tight lipped. JB wasn't talking. Who had won was still anyone's guess.

We had to wait until three o'clock by the time all the other teams, wildly running around New York City, had returned from the urban

jungle. Everybody was in high spirits and the friendship we had cultivated felt true, lasting and warm. The moment of truth was upon us.

"Ladies and gentlemen, can I have your attention please," spoke JB,
"Willis will now reveal the official Human*Race's* final standings." Willis
strolled to the front with his giant list and posted it in front of the
crowded room. With his friendly southern accent, Willis pronounced
without further ado, "It was a great race everybody. Here it is guys. Hail
to the victors."

We had won the race!

We had actually won the race.

As Tom Wolfe put it, we had become *Masters of the Universe*. Well, at
least the world!

Someone immediately asked us what we were gonna do with the
$20,000 in prize money. Andy and I looked at each other smiling for a
brief nanosecond and, knowing that the cameras were rolling, we replied
"We're going to *Disneyland!*" Actually, to my great embarrassment and
for some still unknown reason, Andy, my great teammate who had obviously cracked by this time, uttered the infamous words, "...I thought
there would be some smooth hairless boys to go with this check!" Pure
shock effect, but the horror on the two *Visa International* exec's faces was
all too obvious as polite, uncertain laughs filled the room.

The Del Ray Boys, who had worked so hard just to stay afloat, had
placed second winning themselves $10,000 for their blood, sweat and
tears. Kevin and Mitchell, our ever-so-brief partners in cultural crime
during the New York portion, had won $5,000 by placing third. All in
all, most everybody was happy with the results. Everybody cheered and
clapped for each team as they were announced, introduced and presented
with their winnings. A few pictures of Andy and I were taken with JB,
Willis and other event organizers, along with some of the corporate
sponsors. Finally, a big oversized *VISA* travelers check, that I was sure
we'd have trouble cashing later, was handed to us. The irony of it all is
that we exclusively used *American Express* travelers checks throughout

the entire trip. Andy immediately tried to pocket his winnings trying to jam the check in his pants. We were both on cloud nine.

A party was to be held in all the Human*Racer's* honor that evening around eightish. "We'll be there with bells on," we happily told JB and Willis. We took the money and ran. It had all happened so fast. A lot like the last seventeen days around-the-world.

We all met for a final grand feast that brisk New York evening at the *Marriott Marquis*. Now that the Human*Race* was officially over, many of the competitors swapped some wildly hilarious war stories about personal trials and tribulations while on the road. Things they did and didn't do along the way. Most were horror stories. Even still, it was clearly obvious, now that the race was but a memory, that we were all suffering from fond afterglow's of our adventure. A screenplay writer could have had a field day listening to the wacky and sublime tales. Interesting stories relating to personal hardships, newfound friendships, personal growth by overcoming mental and physical obstacles, numerous cultural clashes, and an ultimate overriding sense of humility. It definitely has the makings of a boffo action-adventure filled dramedy. Add a little romance to it, (Maybe with some conflicted nuns!?) and you'd get a highly combustible box office blockbuster opening weekend movie with definite legs.

Knowing that instant nostalgia is surely the cheapest and most contrived of our human emotions, Andy and I made no promises to see other team members in the future. We didn't even suggest doing lunch once. We exchanged no phone numbers and took no addresses. We just faded into the cold Manhattan night air and partied till dawn. For now, the Human*Race* chapter of our lives was over. Our professional *raison d'être* had been achieved. We would now attempt to return to real life. We had women to do and places to go.

.

Back to the Rat Race

As I recall the adventure we had, I truly understand that what we did was basically a very frivolous pursuit in the larger scheme of things and not to be taken too seriously. It was, after all, just a game. But nonetheless, for about three weeks we took a leave of absence from the habitually mundane and trivial aspects of our normal daily lives. Which at times, is itself, sometimes taken way too seriously. We had opted for a wild, non-stop and lively reality check tour of the global village in which we humbly reside. It really is a very small and extremely accessible world out there. Full of dazzling scenic beauty and mystifying cultural diversity.

The Human*Race* helped us to better understand the fundamental common denominators that infect, and affect, all of the 5.2 billion people on our small blue planet. Love of music is clearly universal, as of course is laughter. A simple friendly smile goes a long way in each and every corner of the world. Speaking at times is wholly unnecessary! And clearly everybody is holding out hope for a better and brighter future. Love, and love of children, as seems obvious to all, are the two basic fundamental realities of our existence here on earth. We had enriched our own lives by experiencing the lives, albeit ever so briefly, of the many others who we had crossed paths with. Clearly our continent-hopping outward chase for tacky tourist trophies and postcard-like photo-ops had enabled us to undertake an inward journey to explore our human spirit.

We lived on the edge for a short time and it felt good. We were alive. We traveled on a physical adventure of the mind, where our global literacy was continually under assault and ultimately tested. We apparently passed the test with flying colors. We had overcome bouts of chronic fatigue, self-induced fasting that caused mild hunger pangs, severe jet lag, logistical snafus, bad weather, unexpected transportation glitches, language barriers, mental gridlock, and many of our own basic human frailties. Certainly not the least of our numerous obstacles was the intense and able competition put forth by our fellow competitors. Stamina, self confidence, endurance, humor, flexibility, patience and resourcefulness, were the keys to our ultimate success. I found in myself an inner strength that pushed me to succeed to the degree that I was challenged.

We had been allowed to live out a fantasy of sorts. We had truly learned that no matter where you go, there you are. And discovered, along the road of endless possibilities, that anything truly can happen. We had, for a very short time, followed that glittering yellow brick road. We left our footprints and fingerprints all over the place. And we also collected a colorful bag full of experiences and tales to share with our children and grandchildren. A suitcase full of sometimes tacky treasures, but a mind full of fond memories. My memory bank was once again full. We had gained some additional wisdom about our own human nature. We were indeed richer for the experience.

Top Human*Race* Memories
Scaling Cemetery Walls, Chambery
Train Fire, Sahara Desert
Post-Earthquake Destruction, San Francisco
Karnak Temple, Luxor
Tanah Lot Temple, Bali
Borobudur Temple, Java
Steak and *Frites* Dinner, Paris
Singing School Kids on Tram, Penang
Terraced Rice Paddies, Ubud
Andy's Winning Remark, New York City

Having personally admired and idolized the great explorers of the past like: Leif Erikson, Marco Polo, Alexander the Great, Magellan, Lewis & Clark, Darwin and Dr. Livingston, among others, I took part in this wacky expedition with a certain sense of romantic idealism. Call it a highly personal rite of passage of sorts for me. Graduating from tourist to traveler. And from Boy Scout to global adventurer. No future trip for me will ever be the same. Nothing could ever compare.

Most people complain about the trials and tribulations of traveling these days. Preferring for the most part, in this the age of technofetishes, to travel by means of the *USS Enterprise's* transporter room. Quick. Convenient. And wholly without adventure. Robert Louis Stevenson once said, "For my part, I travel not to go anywhere, but to go. I travel for travel's sake. The great affair is to move." It's true, that for the most part, our special journey was indeed a state of mind. Movement itself became our sole focus.

During our trip around the world we discovered for ourselves the true meaning of our newfound friend Leonardo da Vinci's famous quote, "If you seek knowledge, go to the spring not the fountain." We could just as easily have read yet another travel adventure book cocooned in our comfy beds or watched a *National Geographic* travel video on cable, America's *I-V* tube to the world, or looked through yet another picturesque travel magazine, and passively experienced the places that we would ultimately visit. "Boy Borobudor looks interesting doesn't it dear?" Or "Geez, someday I'd love to ride a camel by the pyramids…maybe someday…" Someday indeed!

Instead, we went out into the world and actively sought out unknown adventures in equally unknown and surprising places. Life is truly too short. We found out for ourselves that the truth unfolds itself through personal experiences alone. The always illuminating *aha* of insight or the bright smile from a strange face was all we really required to keep us moving forward on our divine mission. That's what travel, any kind of travel, does to you.

Traveling like we did, with full reckless abandon, kept our minds alert and our souls alive and young. Experiencing brief fear-induced adrenaline rushes, only adds to the delight of it, after the fact of course! Although we encountered no truly death-defying risks on our parts, it was a risky adventure in and of itself. Especially for our professional careers and personal relationships. Excitement came through participating in the competition and the spirit we tried to embody throughout it's duration. We got to smell many of the world's most beautiful and fragrant rose bushes, albeit ever so briefly. We also got pricked a few times too. But each and every sunrise we witnessed was sacred. And each and every sundown we were graced with viewing, we truly enjoyed and thanked our lucky stars for being able to experience it.

Somewhere along the 40,000 mile race course, we also debunked a few travel related myths that we've heard widely circulated over the years. Firstly, that the grass is always greener on the other side. As true in life as it is in travel. Each place we visited offered us something uniquely special. It had its own personality. Its own secret charms. And if we were so inclined, we indulged in it's strange allure. We fell in love, over and over again. Just go anywhere you have an affinity for and I'm absolutely certain its special characteristics and charms will engross you, and consume your passions.

Secondly, it really doesn't matter how long you spend somewhere. A day, a week, a month or a lifetime. It's what you do with your time when you're there that's important. If you're visiting for just a week and sit and wait for something to happen to you, something eventually will. You'll get bored! But, if you're there for but a single day and go out into your new environment exploring its many possibilities, you'll inevitably find something special. During several of the conversations we had with the locals we met along the way, we learned that many of them hadn't ever visited many of the places in their own backyards! Oddly enough, they were there for a lifetime, and we were strangers in a strange land, just passing through.

And finally, we abandoned the greatest travel myth of all time that says that *"Getting there is half the fun."* It's a big lie! Well, maybe it was true when wagon trains and tall ships were in vogue, but in the jet age of today, getting there is just a minor, sometimes a major, inconvenience. You climb into this long shiny silver metal tube. They seal you in and strap you down. Ply you with bad food, second-rate movies, infectious pillows and supply you with extremely unhealthy oxygen. And presto. Two, three or maybe even fourteen hours later you're there. Airplane travel offers no real challenges anymore, except in getting a seat on your desired flight, and maybe a cabin-class upgrade. But it's a double-edged sword to be sure because we do indeed get to go places we probably never would even think about going to by wagon train or tall ship. Getting there is no longer half the fun, but getting to go there is.

About three weeks after my life returned to some semblance of normalcy, (Well, as normal as it possibly can get in La-La Land!) while I was giving my hundredth telephone interview on the subject of the HumanRace, an *AP* reporter asked me a couple of basic, and ever so redundant questions like, "Would I do it again? And if so, just how would you better prepare yourself for the competition next time?" After a long moment's hesitation, I replied that I would indeed do it again. "We are after all," I boastfully acknowledged some members of the press had called us "the world's greatest travelers!" (We doubt it, but it is fun hearing it!) I continued the interview. Picking up a full head of steam by now, with what my girlfriend said was pure boyish enthusiasm, "And besides…I hear that next year JB and his band of travel agents are planning on sending us to Kashmir to partake in yak races. And from there I hear we'll be off to the Beirut suburbs of Bekkaa Valley, no doubt for the weekly running of the tanks. I also hear that Chernobyl, Belfast, and Tierra del Fuego, most likely to get a picture of a penguin, will all be on the HumanRace II 1990 itinerary. We couldn't very well miss out on all that action and adventure now could we?"

As for the how would I better prepare myself question. I told the reporter jokingly that I'd do just a couple of things differently, "First, I'd gain about fifteen pounds. Next I'd visit Tijuana, 'the world's most visited city,' just prior to departure to hone up on my tourist trophy haggling and acquisition skills, while at the same time getting reacquainted with those *Third World Blues* issues of abject poverty, scandalous greed, official bureaucratic corruption and unregulated taxis." Then I told him that, "I'd also take along some *Rollerblades* and buy all my clothes on the road. Packing essentially nothing." And finally, I told him rather tongue-in-cheek, "I'd ask to have my contract renegotiated." Because it seems that the Human*Race* and I have some severe artistic differences. But that's another story for another interview session.

Speaking of the *Fourth Estate*, I've become aware of the fact that journalists have written about us from all over the world, and that's without the benefit of the services of a high-priced publicity agent on our parts! Writers were contacting us all the time. Once I even got a call at 3:47 a.m. from an *"AM Sydney"* radio show asking me if I'd be on the show the following morning. I passed on the opportunity to get heckled across the Pacific for ten minutes with an Aussie morning drive time shock jock, but Andy did it. One night while on a ski weekend in Park City, Utah, Andy's happy face suddenly appeared on a cable show while I was channel-surfing. He was doing a *Travel Channel* interview. It was surreal seeing him talk about our trek. The interviewee just didn't quite grasp the craziness of it all.

Misinformation was rampant though. One Canadian article had me living in San Diego working as "some kind of executive." Others labeled me either as an "LA businessman" or "corporate assistant." *GEO Magazine*, the French version of *National Geographic*, listed me as a "spy novelist." Because of Andy's comedy world celebrity status we were even written about in a New York City society magazine. Our names were right there along side Steven Speilberg, Steve Martin, Kevin Kline, Joe Papp, Sydney Pollack and Liz Smith! My two sisters were impressed but very confused. It took a lot of explaining on my part to get my foreign friends to understand anything about my "real life."

Something weird happened a few months later while I was sitting on an *American Airlines* jet bound for Key West, the lady next to me was reading the inflight magazine and an article about me and Andy's crazy trip. The piece was entitled *"Hunting for Mozart's Hair"* and portrayed us as a clairvoyant old gay couple—which we're not! After reading it she tilted her head up and turned to me saying, "Boy that was a crazy story." I leaned over noticing what she'd just read and replied, "Lady, you don't know the half of it!"

Other trip tidbits and pieces cropped up in *Self Magazine, Travel & Leisure, Outside Magazine* and dozens of newspapers from Hong Kong's *Sunday Morning Post* to *The Tennesseean*, from the Toronto *Globe & Mail* to *Orange County Register*.

Over the last few months, several interesting developments have occurred in both my partner Andy's life and my respective life. So a status report update is called for.

Andy, now in addition to doing his stand up comedy routines in Manhattan and working on his feature article writing projects, has begun working with the *Travel Channel*. In addition to being an on-the-air talent with his beautiful co-host Willow Bay, he's also producing his own show called *"Video Escapades."* It offers the viewer some pretty incredible travel stories ala *"America's Funniest Videos."* Needless to say, I offer my input on occasion whenever asked. Andy's happy in New York City and is looking forward to our next, yet to be determined, yearly travel adventure. Recently, I'm proud to say, that Andy had an op-ed piece published in the *New York Times*.

On a personal note, an ancient African proverb says, *"To be sure your friend is a friend, you must go with him on a journey. Travel with him day and night. Go with him near and far…"* Through both trials and tribulations, Andy has proved over and over again that he is my good friend. And he always will be…

Closer to home, I got married for the first time in that neon oasis of Las Vegas to that tall leggy Icelandic gal in early December 1989. And after getting back to work and my daily routine, and watching the *Lakers* season unfold, I began wondering about my next Grand Adventure.

And so I day dream about where my next trip will take place. I'll visit Iceland next Summer to meet with my new Viking relatives in Reykjavik. Iceland, the great exporter of cod and *Miss Worlds*, and from the mainland I plan on visiting the rocky puffin-laden volcanic island of Vestmannaeyjar…

Another volcano story! That's where this tale started didn't it? Once upon a time a long time ago in the mountainous jungles of Java. Well, this is where it ends too.

The HumanRace 1989

A Concise and Slightly Abridged Version:

26 October: LAX-SFO
  SFO-HNL-HKG
  Cross International Date Line (Miss one day)
28 October: Do Hong Kong (6 hours)
  HKG-SIN (Airport Boogaloo)
  SIN-KUL
29 October: KUL-MEL via the Meleka Express
  MEL-KUL
  KUL-PEN
30 October: PEN-KUL
  KUL-SIN
31 October: Do Singapore (4 hours)
  SIN-JKT
  Midnight at the Oasis
01 November: JKT-JOG
  Do Yogjakarta (6 hours)
  JOG-DPS via the People's Express
02 November: Do Bali (5 hours)
  Shower, Eat, Sleep and Drink…
03 November: Do Bali again (42 hours)
04 November: BBQ and Floorshow with the Prince of Ubud
05 November: DPS-JKT

JKT-SIN

5th Place: 4 hours, 37 minutes and 2 seconds behind leaders?!

SIN-CAI

06 NOVEMBER: CAI-ALX (Train Station Boogaloo)

Do Alexandria (2 hours)

ALX-CAI

CAI-LUX via the Nile Express

Bad fire. Really bad fire.

07 NOVEMBER: Do Valley of the Kings (4 hours)

LUX-CAI

Do Cairo (7 hours)

08 NOVEMBER: Do Cairo again (42 hours)

3rd Place: 10 hours, 8 minutes and 4 seconds behind leaders?!

10 NOVEMBER: CAI-PAR

Do Paris (2.5 hours)

PAR-CHA via the TGV Bullet Train

Oh where, oh where, has Leonardo's grave gone?

11 NOVEMBER: CHA-MIL

Do Milan (2 hours)

MIL-VER

Do Verona (45 minutes)

VER-VEN

Do Venice (2.5 hours)

12 NOVEMBER: VEN-LJB

The Yugoslavian Black Hole

LJB-SZA

SZA-VEN (via our savior Nico)

13 NOVEMBER: VEN-MIL

MIL-JFK

Elapsed Time: 17 days, 15 hours and 45 minutes

(Do not try this yourself! We are professionals....)

14 NOVEMBER: Sleep

15 NOVEMBER: Eat and Sleep
16 NOVEMBER: Eat, Drink and Sleep
17 NOVEMBER: Do NYC (5 hours)
　　1st Place Winners of HumanRace
　　40,000 miles....
　　5,000 years of history.....
　　106 scavenges....
　　22 cities.....
　　9 countries.....
　　4 continents......
　　2 songs......
　　1 strange round-the-world passage in time...

Printed in the United States
24197LVS00005B/91